CONTEMPORARY
DESIGNERS'
OWN GARDENS

CONTEMPORARY
DESIGNERS'
OWN GARDENS

BARBARA BAKER

GARDEN • ART • PRESS

For Robin

FRONT COVER: Dan Pearson's garden, see pp.122-3 (photo: Huw Morgan)
BACK COVER: Isabelle Greene's garden, see p.81 (photo: Marion Brenner)
FRONTISPIECE: Ludwig Gerns' garden, p.55 (photo: Robin Baker)
FRONT ENDPAPER: Andy Sturgeon's garden, see p.181 (photo: Barbara Baker)
BACK ENDPAPER: Fernando Caruncho's garden, see p.31 (photo: Robin Baker)

British Library Cataloguing-in-Publication Data
A catalogue record for this book is
available from the British Library

MIX
Paper from
responsible sources
FSC
www.fsc.org   FSC® C104723

Printed and bound in China
for Garden Art Press, an imprint of the Antique Collectors' Club Ltd., Woodbridge, Suffolk

CONTENTS

INTRODUCTION

'It isn't that I don't like sweet disorder, but it has to be judiciously arranged.' These telling words were written by Vita Sackville-West, poet, author and gardener (1892–1962). Fulfilling this dictum is the task of every garden designer and, if done well, the result will be beautiful, sustainable and resonant; it will provoke an emotional response and satisfy the client's brief. In their own personal plots, garden designers are freed from this last constraint and are able to create a space that need please them alone. In doing so, they inevitably create gardens that reveal much more about themselves.

This book offers the reader a peek into an intimate, hidden world, and a rare opportunity to share the designers' private visions. If the designer's garden is open to visitors, to some extent the public is the client, so none of the gardens included here are generally open. When I visited Antonio Perazzi in his home in

Italy, he said that whilst in London, he had met renowned garden designer John Brookes. Perazzi believes Brookes to be an excellent teacher and professional, with a great sense of composition. However, when Antonio visited Denmans, Brookes' own garden in Sussex, he thought it no different from the gardens Brookes designs for clients and he was disappointed. As Perazzi concedes, Denmans (like, for instance, the garden in Hummelo belonging to Piet Oudolf) is essentially a show garden, rather than a personal one.

Another criterion for choosing whom to include in this book was that they should all be professional garden designers. This does not exclude landscape designers or landscape architects – terms often used, particularly abroad, to encompass designing corporate, institutional and public, as well as private, gardens.

However, it does exclude artists or sculptors who have designed a few gardens, as well as gardeners (such as Monty Don) who do not design for clients. The majority of the designers included here were trained in landscape architecture as well as horticulture, though Tony Smith, Ted Smyth, Made Wijaya and Ute Wittich are all, remarkably, untrained.

The featured designers are amongst the most successful and accomplished working today and are at the forefront of international contemporary design. However, this is a personal selection and, naturally, it cannot be comprehensive. Each designer chosen is innovative, influential and varied in style. The array of possibilities explored by these twenty designers is extraordinary, but the question that remains is: What are their home gardens like? In contrast to the cobbler whose children go barefoot, these designers' commissioned gardens, as well as their own, are inspirational and relevant. They range from the gardens of Caruncho and Gerns, who draw on geometric, classic lines with masterful, inventive twists; the fanciful, sculptural garden of Cullity; the startling ingenuity of Blanc and Geuze; the tropical

theatricality of Wijaya; to the plant-led collaboration with nature that is Perazzi's personal plot.

Garden styles have evolved throughout the world for different reasons, but recent times have seen exceptional diversity and change. Materials, rather than plants, are the essential tools of many contemporary landscape designers, and new materials and technologies become available all the time, creating new aesthetics (seen particularly in the work of Gerns, Smyth and Woodhams). Some designers with naturalistic concepts are experimenting with plants, prolonging the planting period and capturing the wilderness in a structured way. Jens Jensen (1860–1951) took his inspiration from the prairies in America to mix perennials with grasses in his gardens. This idea was taken up fifty years later by Oehme van Sweden, and then by Oudolf, Pearson, Perazzi, Stuart-Smith and many more.

OPPOSITE: Ludwig Gerns' garden.

BELOW: Antonio Perazzi's garden.

Tension, between the powerful or invigorating and the poetic or peaceful, and between wild nature or openness and artificial order or enclosure, always produces innovation (for example in Caruncho and Masuno). There is a contemporary emphasis on analysing the site, the spirit of place, and of tampering with nature as lightly as possible (seen in the work of Greene, Pearson, Perazzi and Wirtz). At the other extreme, new ideas, incorporated into conceptual gardens, environmental art and temporary gardens, for instance, result in provocative, avant-garde horticultural narratives (such as those by Cullity, Geuze and Tony Smith). As innovation is embraced, gardens have become more individual and their design has also become an important means of self-expression.

The role of the garden designer has long existed, yet only recently, with the acceptance that art may be ephemeral, has it been considered beside other creative artists, with great gardens being acknowledged as works of art. But contemporary gardens should be viewed in context. In Western art, the term 'modern' has become indentified with the Modernist movement of the 1930s and more recently with Post-Modernism. Modernism, especially in architecture, rejected decoration and ornament. Post-Modernism challenged this, particularly functional design. Now, a similar wave of experimentation is affecting garden design, though in Asia there is still more careful reference to tradition.

Garden design today tends to be increasingly concerned with form, spatial manipulation, land art and allegory. There is a strong focus on the idea that gardens should reflect people's response to both the land and contemporary culture. Instead of being seen as colourful decoration, or trophies, plants are increasingly used by designers to enhance atmosphere. As Made Wijaya playfully writes in *Tropical Garden Design,* 'a garden is much more than the sum of its plants'. He continues: 'A well-composed garden, tropical or otherwise, first complements the architecture or landscape to which it is attached, then creates a story – what the Japanese call a *tagachi* or "point of view" – that involves all the elements, the path, ponds, outdoor furniture, accents and lighting.'

All these components, as well as plants, are creatively deployed by the designers in this book in both their own and their clients' gardens. In addition, these gardens have something more. Fletcher Steele, an American landscape architect (1885–1971) stated that 'the chief vice of gardens is to be merely pretty'. Outstanding gardens shock, surprise and delight; they conjure memories, heighten senses and create a feeling of otherworldliness. It is fascinating to discover what these personal plots mean to their owners, how these gardens are used, and in what ways they differ from, or are similar to, their commissioned work.

Very few garden designers become wealthy from their chosen career. Their own gardens, in the main, are smaller than those of their clients and the money they can spend on them is less. This enables designers, in some cases, to fulfill their visions in gardens that are not their own, but this does not diminish their personal plots in any way. As in other art forms, such as poetry, music, sculpture or dance, certain restrictions are often what produce the most powerful results.

Private gardens are special. The owner knows this space more intimately than any other, and is able to see it grow, develop and change in different years, seasons and lights. In a home garden, the user is aware of the small things which subtly alter the relationships between neighbouring shapes. Being this familiar with a plot is a singular experience.

In their book, *Gardens of the Future,* Guy Cooper and Gordon Taylor quote Jacques Wirtz as having said "I cannot really believe in a designer who does not live in a garden". Yet, remarkably, some prestigious landscape designers do not at present have their own garden. Amongst these are Andy Cao, Luciano Giubbilei, Raymond Jungles, Paul Martin, Jack Merlo, Roberto Silva and Vladimir Sita, who sent me this wonderful email in response to my request to include him in my book:

> Dear Barbara,
> I think that you would need to leave my page blank. My garden exists only in my imagination and it keeps changing all the time. There may be hundreds of alternatives – some of them drawn and existing in unknown places. I am a garden parasite, I have many gardens, they belong officially to somebody else and I don't need to touch any dirty soil. Some clients are now my friends and I visit regularly to change, interfere, rip, criticize and also to share some nice drop originated in Oz cellars with them.
>
> I never had a garden in my life if you don't include my vegetable patch in then Czechoslovakia or a few pot plants on the balcony here in Sydney. I call it an orphanage as all plants there are found or grown from seeds that I have inserted in another already occupied pot, like a cuckoo, and forgotten about. There is an odd tomato or chilli plant and parsley, images of which would destroy your book.
>
> So I apologise for not being able to help you. With kind regards, Vladimir.

How many of us have virtual gardens in our minds? Most designers, nevertheless, find great pleasure being in their own earthly gardens. Some go as far as to say that their garden is essential to them. Many designers use their own plots for experimentation (amongst them Cullity, Geuze, Greene, Stuart-Smith, Perazzi and Wirtz). Others, such as Fogarty and Masuno, find their gardens relaxing or enjoy family life in their outdoor spaces, as do Guinness, Lutsko and Smith in particular.

Naturally, every garden is different and each is imbued with a unique atmosphere, but three designers whose own gardens bear pronounced similarities to their commissioned work are Cullity, Gerns and Woodhams. Some of the private gardens featured in this book are very different to the ones created for clients. These include the personal plots belonging to Blanc, Fogarty, Lutsko, Pearson, Smith, Smyth, Sturgeon, Wijaya and Wittich. The majority of the designers' styles are recognisable, whether displayed in their personal or commissioned gardens, but in their own plots, they frequently feel free to indulge themselves more. They allow more self-seeding, employ less strict discipline, take greater risks and often accept the need for higher maintenance. What is true about all of these varied personal plots is that they more clearly reflect the character, passion and philosophy of their designers.

All who participated in this project are owed huge thanks. They each gave up a lot of time in their very busy schedules to candidly discuss their gardens and allow a privileged and deeply rewarding view of their personal plots. Their gardens settled into my imagination and inspired me in my own garden, as I hope they will you, too.

ABOVE: Antonio Perazzi's garden.

BELOW: Jacques Wirtz's garden.

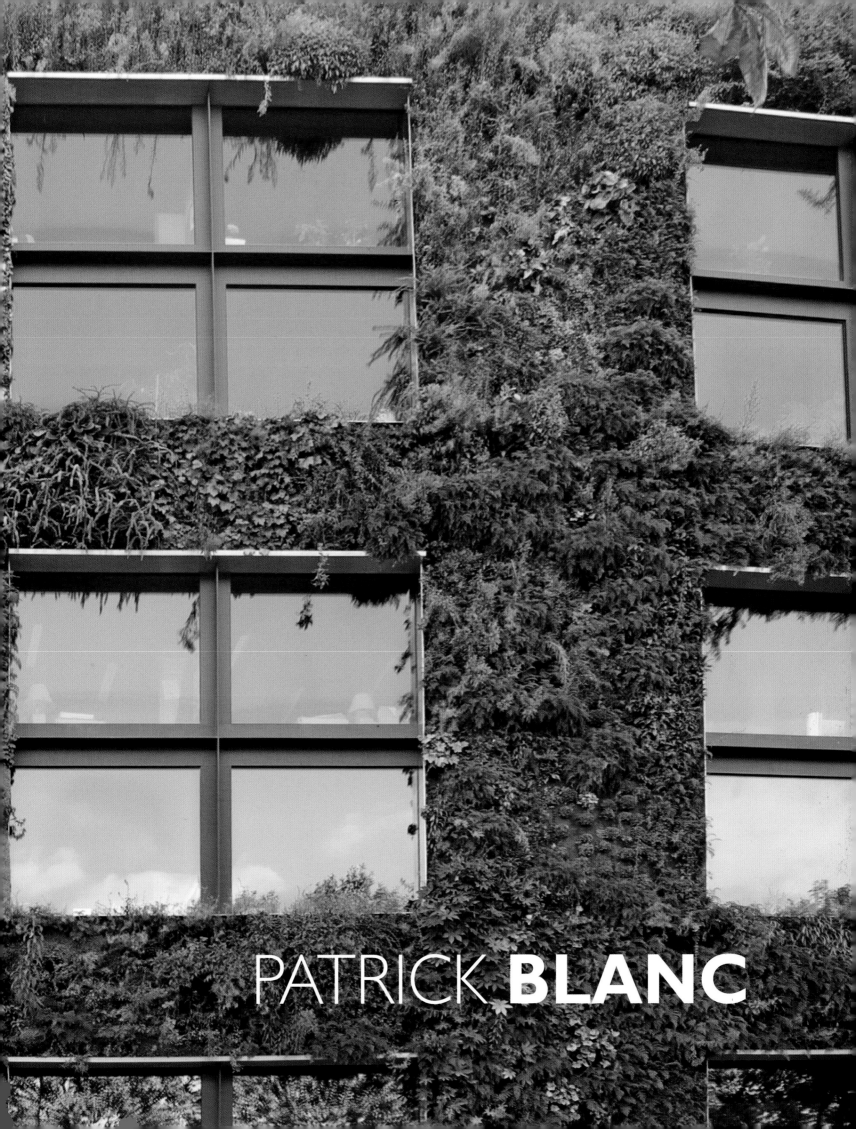

PATRICK **BLANC**

A visit to Patrick Blanc's private garden in Paris is an experience never likely to be forgotten.

Patrick Blanc is renowned throughout the world for his vertical gardens: walls covered with plants (see pp.10-11, 20-21). His method involves a durable metal frame which is held a few inches away from the wall (allowing air circulation and not causing weight on the wall). The frame is covered with PVC and then non-biodegradable felt; plants such as ferns, mosses, flowers, climbers and shrubs are inserted into the felt without soil, and are then fed by irrigated water containing added nutrients.

From the age of fifteen, Patrick began experimenting with growing tropical plants on his bedroom wall in his parents' apartment. After many misadventures with floods, decomposing substrates and undesirable smells, he found success with a process similar to the one he still uses. He first tried the system outside about fifteen years later. In 1991 he moved to a rented house in the suburbs of Paris and realised that the living room looked out onto a plain concrete wall. Soon after, the outdoor vertical garden, using temperate plants, was born. When I ask if his was the first, he replies: "It seems so. No one, anywhere in the world, has said anything different."

Patrick's gardens now bring both greenery and artistry to public and private urban places around the globe – from museums to shopping malls, corporate lounges to car parks, and boutiques to bathrooms. His technique has also been imitated or adapted by other designers. Commenting on the incredible number of vertical gardens at recent Chelsea Flower Shows, he says: "It is good. I cannot cover all the walls of the world by myself! Some are successful; others less so." What is certain is that Patrick's influence has introduced a whole new concept in garden design. One can know this, and one can see many of his astounding living walls, but nothing prepares you for the wow factor of visiting Patrick Blanc's own home in Paris.

From entering through a dreary, unprepossessing façade, I was transported into a different world. The fact that Patrick found this house is remarkable. What he has done with it is miraculous.

Entering the house there is a central courtyard, where three of the walls are covered with plants; crossing this and stepping inside, there is an open-plan kitchen, dining room, seating area and study. The back wall is cloaked in plants. At its base is a huge tank of water (20,000 litres) and covering the majority of this is an enormous sheet of glass (6 x 7 metres), forming the study floor. On top of the glass is Patrick's desk, 'floating' on an aquarium in which fish live happily. To one side, a staircase leads up to a bedroom, music studio, open-air shower and small bathroom with a planted wall. Throughout one can hear birdsong, for bright, tropical birds live in the green wall inside the house.

It is 11 a.m. and Patrick asks if I will join him in a glass of white wine. When I decline and ask for some water he feigns shock, saying, "Water is for plants, not for human beings!" He is petite and lively with emerald green hair and fingernails three centimetres long. I am reminded both of a pixie and of Chinese scholars who traditionally grew the fingernails on their smallest (fifth) finger long to prove that they did not do manual labour – but Patrick is a gardener. He is, admittedly, also a researcher at the French National Centre for Scientific Research (where he has worked for 28 years), an expert in tropical rain forests (with an intimate knowledge of plant growing conditions when deprived of light in the shadow of trees), an artist and a modern day plant-hunter.

He and his long-term partner, Pascal Heni (a singer), have lived in this house near Porte de Choisy since June 2009. They looked for a property for a year and chose this one because they liked the floor (concrete with a pattern of gravel in it) and the structure. In fact, they changed hardly anything except for adding bookshelves, the vertical gardens and the aquarium floor. Patrick claims not to be interested in architecture or in having to do a lot of interior decorating. He explains that the courtyard was ugly, but he saw the possibility of having large vertical gardens both indoors and out. Another attraction was the small terrace upstairs, which leant itself perfectly to an outside shower; Patrick always uses this one, even in winter when it is snowing – the indoor one is for Pascal.

Patrick's interests, since he was aged five and sat in his doctor's waiting room, fascinated by an aquarium, have not changed: fish, plants and water. His private garden, combining these, is purely for pleasure. In his courtyard, Patrick decided not to cover all of the walls, deliberately leaving one bare, to see the structure of the house. His aim is always to show some of the existing façade of a building rather than to swamp it. He is keen to enhance architecture, not to hide it, and for his gardens to work in unison with buildings.

Patrick wanted his own courtyard to be light with fairly large-leafed plants, in contrast to inside. It is edged with a gulley of warm water (a heat pump is hidden in a cupboard in the wall), covered by a metal grid, below which tropical fish swim amongst underwater plants. One of these is a cryptocoryne, a plant first seen and loved by Patrick in books when he was a teenager, and eventually witnessed on a field trip to Borneo in 2005, where they were growing by the thousands in the swampy zones of the understory of the Gunung Mulu National Park. Here, in his garden, personal plants, textures and reflection all play important roles, as does the merging of inside and out. There is much glass and many windows. In summer the doors are always open and meals are taken outside.

Inside, in the aquarium, the water is also heated but, rather like under-floor heating, the energy is not lost and instead provides warmth to the room. Here Patrick has created a more cave-like atmosphere, with many soft plants, such as mosses, as well as bare patches of wall. As with all his walls, but here especially, the structure of each specimen is seen clearly; viewed at eye level or from underneath, the plants reveal themselves from roots, to basal crowns to foliage (almost in the same tradition as the Victorian Europeans who planted 'exotic' conifers on mounds to be viewed from beneath, enabling intimate admiration of the network of roots). Unlike some vertical gardens, Patrick's diaphragms allow the roots of the plant to develop on the surface.

However, the sparse planting here would be totally impossible for a client, Patrick claims. Clients, he says, always want an entire wall totally covered with plants. These are often planted in decorative patterns (which actually imitate nature), typically in long, near-vertical lines or slightly slanted swathes going from bottom left to higher right, whereas in his own garden you see each individual plant clearly against its background. "At home I wanted something very different from what I do in my other projects", Patrick tells me. Both the inside and outside walls are dramatic, accentuated by lighting, but the interior is more calming, and the cave-like aspect (including a small waterfall appearing to run down through rocks) is strangely reminiscent of a troglodyte home.

OPPOSITE ABOVE LEFT: Patrick deliberately leaves some of the courtyard wall unadorned with plants so that the architecture of the building is still visible, acting in harmony with the vegetation.

OPPOSITE BELOW LEFT: The courtyard forms a perfect foil to the indoor space from which it is always visible.

ABOVE RIGHT: Even the indoor shower and bathroom have a glass ceiling and wall through which greenery can be seen.

RIGHT: The outdoor shower, used daily by Patrick, might almost be in Bali.

"It is impossible for me to live without the proximity of plants", states Patrick, "I need the integration of plants with myself and my life. Luckily Pascal likes plants too." Yet Patrick likes jungles and cities, but not gardens! His argument is this: "If you live in a city, you have to decide to take time, or lose time, in order to go into a garden. When you have a vertical garden, you make no decision; it is on your way, on the pavement or by the subway. It is more similar to walking in mountains or jungle and being presented with plants clinging to a cliff by a waterfall and it is spectacular. In a horizontal garden, the guy who makes it decides where you go. He decides the paths, and where you have to sit. A vertical garden is more like a picture, where it is your own eye which decides whether you are more interested in a triangular leaf or a frond."

Although analogies can be made with paintings, Blanc's gardens are living and rather than being static, they evolve. However, there is a contrast between horizontal gardens, where one needs to be constantly working with the plants in a hands-on manner, and vertical gardens which, once set up and with irrigation and nutrients in place, require little further maintenance. Everything is controlled automatically – irrigation three to five times a day (according to season and aspect) and about one tenth of the amount of nutrients normally used in horticulture (added automatically). In yet another respect, however, Patrick's own garden is a bit different from his commissioned ones. At home, he can change a particular plant when he feels like it, and his walls are perfectly maintained, whereas some of his larger public pieces become, periodically, in need of a whole area of replanting.

In theory, anyone can have a vertical garden, and once you have got a tank and a pump, it is quite cheap. Patrick believes that even if you do not live in a city, and own a conventional garden, there are benefits from an indoor vertical garden, which can play a powerful part in creating a new relationship between inside and out. If you were to make a vertical garden that was only 2.5 metres high, it would be relatively easy; however, if, like his own wall, yours is 8 or 9 metres, he warns that if it fell, it could kill you. Additionally, to maintain something up to 8 metres is fine, using a ladder, but if it is far higher, like many of Patrick's commissioned walls, it is quite a problem. One big advantage, of course, is that if it is small, the structure is moveable. Patrick himself has some pieces of felt, for example, where a *Ficus villosa* from Malaysia grows, dating from a previous home in 1982.

Patrick's desk appears to float on the glass floor in possibly the most unusual room I have ever seen.

On the wall behind Patrick's desk is the drooping-fingered favourite *Iris japonica*. Almost all of his walls include this plant, though more often in greater numbers. He says that on the rocks of the understory in Japan and China it forms "long vertical corridors of green hands".

Opposite: At the base of the interior wall is a channel which is not covered by glass, enabling Patrick to feed his tropical fish.

Patrick's own living walls can be compared to a plantsman's garden, where he has favourites, such as plants from the nettle family, with very varied-shaped leaves that are always architectural. He explains that other people like them less because they have no flowers. Although all Patrick's living walls are largely green, they do also contain colour. He likes irises, for example, "because the leaves are like fingers, drooping with long nails, like mine!" and has used them in many of his vertical gardens as a signature plant, ever since he first saw *Iris japonica* hanging from a rock in Japan. At home Patrick can also try plants that he has never tried before and incorporate souvenirs from different countries.

Here, Patrick is able to use rare specimen plants, found in specialist nurseries, individually. Clients would need 50 of the same plants in order to create a design, but for Patrick, virtually each plant tells a story. In his house there are around 600 different plants outside and about 300 inside. So, for a project of around 150 square metres he has used nearly 1000 different plants. For a client, for the same size walls, he would use around 80 to 100 different species. In either case, the many species form an ecosystem. More thuggish plants replace some; elsewhere others might invite themselves in, so the results evolve mysteriously.

The fact that Patrick is a trained botanist helps. He has expert knowledge of subtropical forests as well as temperate zones,

and a keen sense of the way in which plants grow according to the light. So, on his walls, he will mimic the architecture from forest canopy to understory, or from cliff's edge to the dark recesses at its base. He places larger shrubby plants, which require the most light at the top; plants such as buddleja, berberis and cotoneaster, with herbaceous plants such as heuchera, tiarella, campanula and iris below, and then ferns and saxifrages at the bottom. What is perhaps surprising is that even plants such as these, seen commonly in European town gardens, when planted vertically, evoke tropical lushness.

Patrick hopes his plant walls play a part in the well-being of people living in cities. Unlike an ivy-clad wall, his vertical gardens convey "the breath of the wilderness in the midst of the city". He believes that it is through the integration of many species on the same wall that "the imagination is fired up". Plants are chosen according to light, temperature and wind (for example, he is currently working on a building in Sydney which is almost 200 metres high). Yet all the plants within one wall necessarily receive the same amount of water and minerals.

Each project is totally different. In some cases, such as for a school in San Francisco, only native Californian plants will be used. Or for a garden in Bali, it would be no good just to make a list of plants and then find that he could not get them, so he would visit all the remote nurseries to see what was available. In Europe he knows which plants are available, so it

is easier, but Beth Chatto's famous adage, 'the right plant in the right place', applies vertically as well as horizontally. For projects outdoors in Poland or Qatar only a limited number of species will thrive. Indoor walls, however, have the same climate and consistent light levels all over the world; it is always 20 degrees (in Moscow it is heated, in Bangkok it is cooled) and so the same tropical plants can be used. With enough plant knowledge, vertical gardens can exist anywhere in the world, in any situation.

Nowhere else in the world, however, does a botanical tapestry rise from an aquarium, as it does in the study area of Patrick's home. He wanted the bottom of the aquarium (which is 50 centimetres deep) to be the same level as the rest of the floor.

This involved digging down about 30 centimetres, covering 15 centimetres with concrete and still allowing room for underwater plants. These Patrick strokes, by the edge of the aquarium where there is a strip with no glass, so that he can also feed his fish (numbering about 1,000) which he allows to nibble at his fingers. Some of the tropical birds, which nest in the branches above, are insectivores (which is useful, although he also feeds them with larvae), while others eat seeds. There are birds from India, Indonesia and Venezuela but all are bred in Europe. Once or twice, one has flown out by mistake, but mainly they live happily inside, and several have produced chicks.

This indoor wall is immensely tactile. *Ficus villosa* has leaves pressed tightly flat, mosses softly protrude, while ferns feather.

A favourite nettle, growing near the trickling waterfall in the corner, was brought back from Bali – a revelation in non-stinging elegance. From the corner, too, stretches a large branch of a piper (pepper), which serendipitously frames Patrick's desk. Branches die back; new shoots grow. In the opposite corner, an open staircase commences under the water. Climbing to the top, one sees the red leaves of a pandanus, collected by Pascal from Thailand, where he found the seedling in elephant dung. A bird, flashing blue, darts by.

Upstairs one walks through plants in an indoor bathroom to climbers surrounding the outdoor shower, and on to Pascal's studio with desk and piano. Here there is one large potted palm ("because Pascal wanted one plant") beside the original wicker chair from the film *Emanuelle 2*, in which Sylvia Kristel famously lounged topless. But wherever one goes in the house, a living wall is visible. Even though Patrick repeats that he has done little work structurally, the changes he has made to the space, which is an integrated whole – house and garden – make it unique.

ABOVE: A view of the Quai Branly Museum in Paris, where the immense windows add another dimension to this wall, reflecting the street outside, framing views with *Pilea petiolaris, Elatostema umbellatum*, soleirolia and heuchera.

OPPOSITE: The planting for the Rue d'Alsace, Paris, completed in 2008, is a typical Blanc design on a particularly large scale – over 15,000 square metres. This vast vertical garden enlivens a narrow, corridor-like street between the Gare du Nord and Gare de l'Est.

Leaving the house, walking towards the Metro, I am still buzzing. Passing walls covered with graffiti, it occurs that these, too, display decoration or statements, occasionally beautiful, often arresting. Patrick's walls convey a gentler message – in public places, on a grand scale, they stimulate; in his home they are magic.

FERNANDO CARUNCHO

Iridescent ears of wheat, silver-leaved olives and pencil-thin cypresses combine in a perfect paradigm at 'Mas de les Voltes'.

RIGHT: A wonderful allée of olive trees contrasts with the rectangles of wheat in this exceptional 'Wheat Garden'.

PREVIOUS SPREAD: Trademark Caruncho is nonetheless awe-inspiring, displaying man's partnership with the land: something fundamental in his work, here in the garden of a Catalan farmhouse.

Open any book about contemporary garden design and it is almost certain to mention Fernando Caruncho; and with good reason. His gardens are masterful creations that are rivetingly beautiful. So, when I saw his private garden and met Fernando, my expectations were high, but were not disappointed. The garden is fabulous and he is erudite, passionate, self-effacing, gracious and kind, with an infectious chuckle.

Fernando Caruncho, who likes to be called a gardener, rather than a landscape designer, was born in Madrid in 1958. His early love of gardens came from visiting those of his grand-

parents: one in verdant Galicia, the other in arid Andalusia; both were magical places to the young Fernando. Later he studied philosophy at university, where he learnt of the Greek philosophers' use of the garden for teaching – a place where physical and spiritual worlds join. Inspired by the idea that knowledge, gardens and nature are strongly connected, he decided to study landscape design as a means of making philosophy a reality. Since 1980, from his office in Madrid, he has designed numerous internationally venerated public and private gardens in Spain, as well as in England, France, Greece, Italy, the United States, New Zealand and Japan.

Caruncho's designs are sensational yet minimal; visually poetic, yet underpinned by geometry and philosophy; rooted in Spain's Moorish history, but also completely contemporary. He is famed for his focus on grid formation (reflecting Islamic influence) and his skillful manipulation of water and light, which together create harmony and a contemplative mood. His style is exemplified in his masterpiece, 'Mas de les Voltes' ('The Wheat Garden'), created for a traditional Catalan farmhouse in Castel de Ampurdan.

The colours here are limited to gold and different shades of green. The planting is restricted to wheat, grass and trees of strongly contrasting texture and light. The effect is breathtaking. Young green and then golden wheat grows in six rectangles; a grid of lawn paths forms the wheat parterre and is edged with alternating tall, dark cypresses and grey, gnarled olives. From the farmhouse above, the formal pattern is clear; from below one is immersed in a sea of wheat. All the plants are common in

the Mediterranean, but Fernando was the first designer to use agricultural crops in a garden.

Fernando took the landscape of his childhood with his grandmother in Andalusia, and created formality, tranquility and a new aesthetic on a grand scale. With typical modesty and eloquence he declares that he was unaware of his innovation: "When you are in love, the incredible things are in the process. To be a gardener is to be in love with natural elements. The idea was in the place. I was surrounded by wheat; I just introduced the wheat into parterres in the garden. I did not think whether it was new or good – the important thing is to be authentic and then act on it."

Also included in Mas de les Voltes is a serene water parterre, where four brick-edged, wide grass paths enclose flat sheets of water (see pp.22-3). This idea was developed even further in

Water, light, sound and texture combine here, in front of Caruncho's house as well as in the garden behind.

BELOW: The extraordinary, imposing, geometric façade of Fernando Caruncho's house.

This mesmerising parterre at Camp Sarch captures water and clipped escallonia, fluidity and mass, brightness and shadow.

OPPOSITE: Sienna-washed stucco and latticed, rope-like, metal reinforcing bars are used here in Minorca, as well as in Caruncho's own house, courtyard, and pergola.

another of Fernando's iconic gardens, Camp Sarch in Minorca. Traditional Spanish gardens are often viewed from a belvedere; here the central part of this garden is seen from an ochre-washed pavilion with steel rebar grilled windows (not dissimilar from Fernando's own courtyard, see p.30). The spectacular water parterre in Minorca is laid out on a gentle slope. Stone paving forms a net around sixteen squares, some filled with water, others with mounded clipped escallonia (a Spanish equivalent of buxus, used extensively by Caruncho). The still pools reflect trees and shrubs planted nearby, while paths through pines lead to other parts of the garden including a parterre of lemon trees, a lawn with swimming pool and an ancient vegetable garden.

Fernando's own garden, though far smaller in scale, also astounds. Driving northwest of Madrid, one reaches an exclusive housing estate set beside a golf course. The other villas are expensive-looking, but uninteresting. Fernando's house, on the other hand, which he designed himself, is extraordinary. A rectangle planted with silver *Stachys byzantia* (commonly known as lamb's ear) forms a rough carpet in front of the house. Wide stone steps flanked by two rows of sharply

clipped green hedging, lead to a dark, copper-clad door in the centre of a straight, low, long house; its stucco walls washed in burnt Sienna-coloured iron oxide.

The front (which is south facing) has no windows and is both majestic and austere. The large expanse of wall protects the interior from the scorching summer sun and withering winter winds. Along the base of the left hand side is a tank of water, with three brass taps above, like those placed for washing in front of mosques. However, before entering, and viewing the garden, I was taken up the road a few metres to Fernando's studio, also designed by him.

This cool, white, chapel-like building, into which one descends, houses huge scale models of his work. The building has a skylight at the top, reminiscent of the twelfth-century Arabian Baths in Girona (in the province of Catalonia), which Fernando loves. He calls the Baths "a room of light, which is a garden turned to stone". The light in the Baths comes from a domed lantern and fluctuates in a central pool, surrounded by elegant tree-like pillars. There are references to this in Fernando's garden, too.

before you. It is as though you have stepped into a theatre and are looking at the auditorium, but the stage is actually a large, colonnaded, raised, reflective swimming pool, and the seats are hedges, lapping down a slope like the incoming tide. In the centre of these waves is the royal box, in reality a pavilion. What Fernando has unusually chosen to do is to place his house at the bottom of a slope so that you look up at the garden. For him, the garden is paramount and so it resides in pride of place.

The rectangular pool represents about one third of the garden. The planted part thus forms about two thirds of mass to one of void in a seemingly perfect balance. Apart from the clipped hedges of escallonia, a panoply of leaf form and texture is supplied with bamboo, holly, ivy, shrubs and trees, but all is green. The constantly brim-full pool is lined in white, rather than blue, forming a neutral reflective surface. Around its edges are terracotta pots holding citrus and camellia trees. Above the ochre colonnade is a latticed metal grid clothed in wisteria: once a year, its purple, scented plumes hang in the air. Always, the shadows of its branches play on the surfaces below. Beyond, in the courtyard, in which another metal grid separates the garden from the front door, a rose grows. The whole is remarkable, more especially because it is a private garden.

Fernando bought the plot, measuring 25,000 square metres, in 1988, because it gave him the opportunity to build a house facing south (protected to an extent from the severe winters) with a north-facing garden, but as he says, tellingly, "A house is a pretext to live in a garden". His house is actually quite small, with a ground floor and basement (with simple furniture inside arranged in grids). Fernando changed the levels of the plot, using spoil from the pool, so that the floor of the garden pavilion

ABOVE: Looking up from the terrace in front of the glass doors of the living room, one sees the still water of the pool; the calm, comforting cushions of escallonia; and the red pavilion with its skirt of ivy. Most of the garden is seen at once – there is nothing bitty or insubstantial, simply a magnificent whole.

LEFT: Looking out from the pavilion, with its adjustable split-willow blind, the grid over the sitting room window mirrors that of the courtyard. The escallonia echoes the hills, seen over the house roof.

would be exactly the same level as the roof of the house, in order to see the views. Now, if you sit in the pavilion, you look beyond the garden and over the house to mountains and sky. Fernando explains that the pavilion is, in fact, the heart and focus of the garden because it is a place from which to contemplate the landscape and to feel a connection with it. In all his gardens, where possible, this is an essential element.

Light, too, is paramount here. Reflections in the pool are ever-changing, while almost all the plants have shiny leaf surfaces. Though the garden is north-facing, the light in Spain is rich and strong and enables plants to grow well even in this direction. However, there is a short flowering season in Spain, so Fernando maximises the use of evergreen plants. Towards the end of April, the wisteria will flower for a month, the citrus trees will blossom and then the rose blooms. "They mark a moment of splendour," he says, "but this needs to disappear so that the green atmosphere of the garden, together with the water, is in harmony and equilibrium again."

The garden took seven years to develop and build. Fernando was young, without a lot of money at that time. On the plot already were some trees, including 200-year-old oaks, that he

kept, but very little else remained. As he explains, "Having designed a long, flat house, I wanted to emphasise the horizontal plane in the garden as well as to introduce a different level between the garden and the house. The house (being part of the garden) is the first step, then there is the pool and then the planting." Originally Fernando intended to have a sunken pool, level with the paving around the edge, but he raised it when he had a family of two boys, who might fall in. Now, the edge of the pool forms a seat and the columns are higher. He says: "It was a discovery, because it was not in my mind at first, but I am happier with this solution."

Fernando claims that designing his own garden was harder than designing for clients, though his process is always the same. It is essential for him to have a strong affinity and empathy with his clients. He visits a plot many times and takes several months to think about a project before he starts, and then gets an idea based on a point of reference (in the same way that an artist in any media might get inspiration). Then he will do sketches and, finally, a scale model of the house and garden. He might also develop another idea in order to make sure that the first idea was the best. Fernando keeps a close relationship with his clients, continuing to visit them after the project is complete.

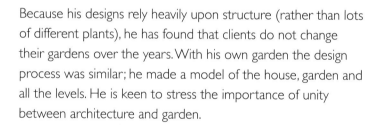

The front door is seen through this grid, which divides the bare courtyard from the garden. Texture, tension and geometry fuse with the placement of a single rose.

RIGHT: A curtain of rustling bamboo backs the amorphous mounds of escallonia, which appear to interlock. In fact, narrow bark paths divide the hedges for maintenance purposes.

Because his designs rely heavily upon structure (rather than lots of different plants), he has found that clients do not change their gardens over the years. With his own garden the design process was similar; he made a model of the house, garden and all the levels. He is keen to stress the importance of unity between architecture and garden.

Grids are also integral to Fernando's work. This is not a new idea but it is an effective one. Squares were fundamental to ancient Egyptian and Roman design. Many Renaissance gardens had rectilinear geometry, as did much Classical and Modernist architecture. In Fernando's garden, grids can be seen literally in the form of metal screens and stucco columns, but also in the axial lines between the house and garden, although here, the whole is softened with planting. In other gardens of his, grids in the form of parterres are sometimes undisguised and are key. Fernando points out that landscape and portrait painters often drew grids on their canvases before starting to paint. As he explains, "The grid is a very simple form of geometry that aids understanding of a space. Unconsciously, I have a perception of the grid. It is a process to understand the place. If you analyse my garden, there is a grid between the relation of the corridors and rooms of the house and the garden. It is like a puzzle to

which the grid gives order. Then, over the years, it is possible to develop more complicated geometries inside the grid."

Fernando's garden is a microcosm of his other work. He, in fact, claims that all his gardens are different and that he does not have a style, so he cannot say whether his own garden is any more different than the others. It is true that all his gardens have different atmospheres and spirits, something that is difficult to convey in photographs. He explains that unlike a piece of art, which is static, gardens are alive and are always moving and transforming with light and reflections. "The ideas for my gardens generate from the place, not from inside me. It is for this reason that I do not like to be called a garden designer or landscape architect, because I don't design anything. I just read the place. It is important not to think too much, but to see and to try to understand. Then you can find the fundamental point of the place. At first this is difficult, but with practice it becomes easier. What I do not want to do is to impose myself on the place. That is terrible and very violent. You need to let the place express its being."

Modestly, Fernando claims that garden design is not a complicated process, but requires patience and clarity. "Simplification is fundamental", he maintains. In the tradition of

Japanese gardens, paring down produces order and calm. As Fernando points out, "Nature is complex but its order is strong and readable. We should not introduce spaces that are very complicated to maintain." His favourite Spanish painter, significantly, is the seventeenth-century artist, Francisco Zurbaran, whose beautifully lit still lives, with geometric compositions, are masterly. Fernando says, "With one lemon, one plate and a piece of bread, he made something incredible. In my own way, I like to be simple too."

Caruncho is often lauded for his inventive and inspirational fusion of the historic and the contemporary, but he rejects this discussion. "I am all the past, my present and my future", he says. "I detest conversations about being contemporary or not. To me the ancient Greeks are younger than modern people. History is our heritage and to go to the future you need the past."

Fernando views his garden as a person with its own personality: "It is a member of the family." For him, perhaps more than any other designer I met, his garden is essential. As he puts it, "It is my home. It is the space where I am free and where it is possible to be myself without any barriers." In life, he says, people are often prevented from being themselves, but

gardens provide that opportunity. He believes that we live a lot in the rational world and yet life is not rational. In his view, "Man is a symbolic animal and in some ways irrational, like nature. To be in a garden is to be in the cycles of nature and gives the opportunity to interpret life in a symbolic way. It is a physical, spiritual and intellectual experience. The rational part of a person has to converge with the irrational part of the garden. Otherwise the rational part of life imbibes the whole of mankind and we lose our origins."

With these views, he naturally spends as much time as possible in his garden, but perhaps surprisingly, he employs a gardener. His two sons, Fernando and Pedro, also help in the garden as they are keenly interested, to the extent that, happily, when they have finished their studies, they will join Fernando in his business. It is they who will have the opportunity to change, or in his words, "renew" the garden, should they wish. For unusually and intriguingly, Fernando believes that his garden is now completely independent from him and is not his responsibility. It is not feasible for him to make changes to it because it has its own identity and is independent. It is like a child; he can help, but not transform his garden.

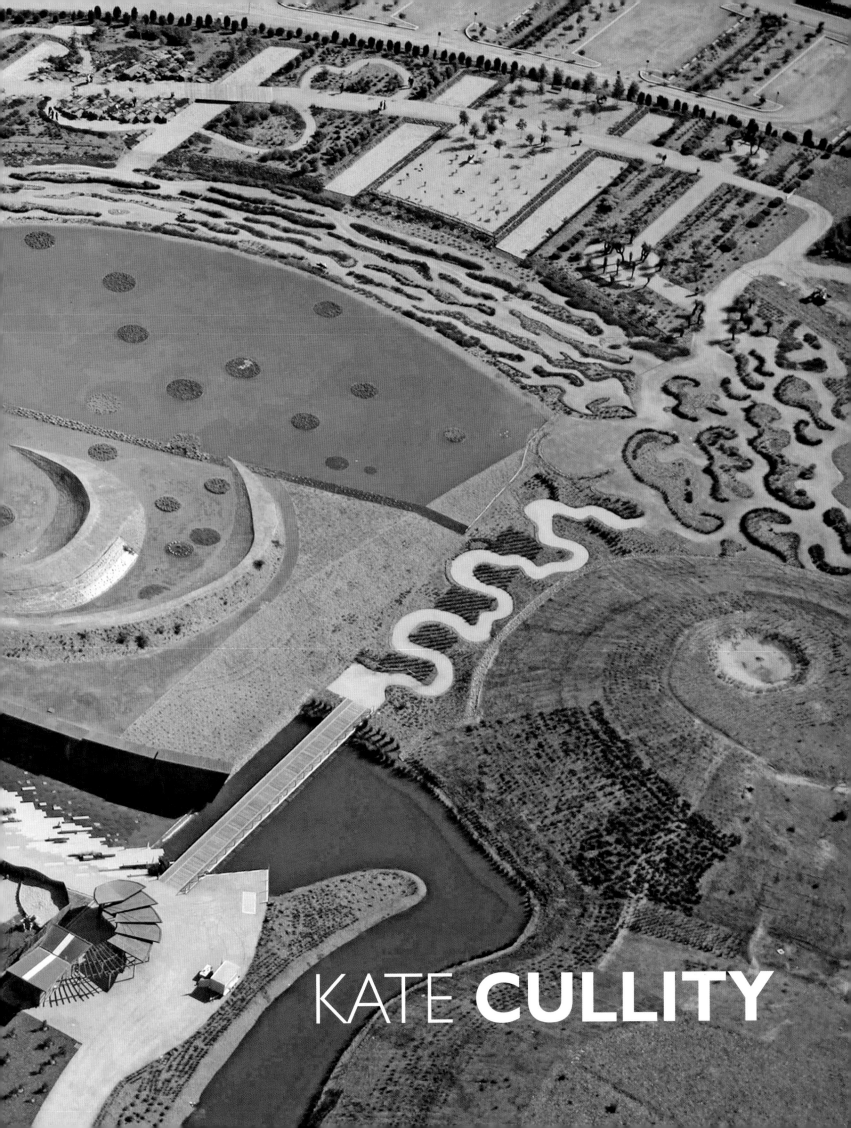

KATE **CULLITY**

PREVIOUS SPREAD: An aerial view of the 'Australian Garden', designed by Taylor Cullity Lethlean with Paul Thompson. In their AILA award submission (which they won) they wrote: 'The design expresses the tension between our reverence and sense of awe for the natural landscape and our innate impulse to change it to make it into a humanly contrived form, beautiful yet our own work.' The same could be said of Kate's garden.

'Desert Space', with its daring use of colour, has clear similarities with the 'Australian Garden'. The 'pictures' within change from time to time, but include a combination of plants and inanimate objects, such as twigs, square blocks of local stones of different heights, angled stone, and small grey balls made from the prunings of cushion bush plant (which Kate thinks too beautiful to throw away).

Kate Cullity's garden, in a residential suburb of Adelaide, Australia, is astonishingly dramatic, and lingers in the mind as a haunting memory long after it has been seen. It is therefore perhaps surprising that it is essentially experimental and even ephemeral, and that despite its arresting quality, for Kate, it is a vital refuge of calm as well as rejuvenation.

The garden weaves around two buildings, where Kate (trained in botany and visual arts) lives with her husband, Kevin Taylor (trained in architecture). They, with the addition of Perry Lethlean (trained in urban design), are the principals of Taylor Cullity Lethlean (TCL), and all share a background in landscape architecture. Their studio-based company expresses the powerful Australian landscape as well as contemporary culture, in poetically conceived sustainable designs. These include award-winning urban waterfronts, national parks, playgrounds, plazas and private gardens. The company often collaborates with fellow designers and artists to create environments characterised by the integration of buildings, artworks and landscape.

Kate started her career in landscape architecture in 1990. She has lived in her present house since 1997, when the garden was very ordinary, with just a few large trees (an apple, an ornamental plum, a silky oak and a Lillly Pilly), a few roses and grass. She and Kevin did not buy the plot for the garden, but because it had a 1900s sandstone villa as well as a contemporary studio – the previous house Kate lived in was bought because it had a huge mulberry tree in the garden. When Kevin and Kate bought this plot, they used the studio for their practice, but the company grew very quickly and moved to new premises within three years.

The garden is approximately 1000 square metres and, it seems to me, could only belong to a garden designer, or possibly be a public space. There was an overall plan, but it was implemented in stages as Kate and Kevin had time, and the garden has also changed as they felt the need to explore different concepts and as Kate added new sculpture. But it has always relied heavily on

structure. Because there are two dwellings and the site is a corner block, Kate says that it lent itself to creating separate gardens, with just glimpses from one to the next. The experience is a bit like walking through the rooms of an art gallery. There are six very distinct areas which, even in their names, suggest the unusual: 'Desert Space'; 'Woven Walls'; 'Still Water'; 'Twisted

Limbs'; 'Ripple Lawn'; and 'Snake in the Grass'. Cohesion is achieved by a repetition of flowing curves and by what Kate describes as "a notion of playing with ideas of frozen movement or the sense of implied movement. I am interested in Kandinsky".

Kate's garden is rare in that it is conceptual, where the idea is as important as the object. As she explains, "I feel that having a strong conceptual underpinning allows us to layer the garden both aesthetically and metaphorically, enabling us to produce something that has more resonance. We are particularly interested in trying to mine the poetic, in the same way as a poet distills down to the essence of things. There are some

A striking, sculpted spine, made by Kate, is suspended from the verandah roof of the house. It is made from sawn eucalyptus roots, which are very hard (Kate broke her saw making it).

Textures and sinuous curves are signature elements in this garden.

OPPOSITE: Even a small garden can be filled with imagination and the enticement to run the stepping-stones or jump the green curves. On top of the interlaced branches and silver grey foliage of *Leucophyta brownii* is a ball of clippings from the same shrub, originally made for a sculptural project, when Kate studied visual arts.

private gardens we have designed where the conceptual has been less important, but it always seems to creep in somehow." In her own garden though, Kate only had to think about herself and Kevin, so it is an indulgence.

'Desert Space' (pp.34-5), a stunning part of their garden, demonstrates conceptualism clearly. Within a perfect oval of bold, red, velvet sand, are about twenty square, abstracted spaces, framed by rusted steel, like pictures or small shrines. These hold plants, sticks, pebbles and other changing exhibits from native and indigenous origins. It is inspired by the experience of walking in the Australian desert, where one is forced to meander between the sparse vegetation. Compacted red sand is used as a metaphor for the continent's interior. Although 'Desert Space' can be walked on (and it is lovely to remove one's shoes and do this), it shares some of the qualities of Zen dry stone gardens (viewed from a platform) where focus heightens observation.

'Woven Walls' curve and intersect in a space adjacent to the main living area of the house, extending it outside. Because the walls are made of concrete, a felicitous result is that in winter, moss grows on them during wet months, transforming them to tactile emerald, complementing the red, jewel berries of nandina which is planted here. Some walls also hold beds of fine and strap-leaved plants, layering texture. Beneath, soft sandstone is intersected with dark, cobbled, radiating lines.

This paving extends into the next garden, 'Still Water', between the back door of the house and the studio. Here, straight dark walls surround reflective water in a raised, rectangular tank and in an oval, stone pool. Flowers, leaves, or berries float in the water; a seasonal snapshot, viewed from the house.

The garden of 'Twisted Limbs' is an extraordinary space of blue-grey movement (see p.42). In front of the studio, branches

and trunks of dwarf blue gums appear to contort in a dance above swirls of festuca grass. Their 'stage' is edged with battens of radial sawn Australian eucalypt and the 'set' also includes an anodised steel bench constructed from bedsprings – another grey element that might bounce into action.

The lovely 'Ripple Lawn' (above) could actually be an entire urban garden in itself. It is a play on the notion of formal hedges, with arcs of tall grass between mown grass, and a sinuous, stepping-stone path curving in counterpoint. Kate got this idea

because she mows the lawns (as Kevin has hay fever) and in her previous house, where they both lived for a while, she started making patterns in the grass. So the arcs are the width of a lawn mower. Although the design is strong, it is softened by colour and texture, as well as informal native and Mediterranean planting.

'Snake in the Grass' (see p.36 left) is adjacent to Kate's studio. In fact it is the opposite of its name, in that a precisely cut snake (made of native lomandra – a tussock-forming perennial with flat leaves, here clipped at one height) weaves diagonally through a bed of sandstone gravel. This garden was directly inspired by the Zen gardens of Kyoto, and is intended to create a contemplative experience when entering and leaving the studio. Another snake hangs nearby. This is an S-shaped sculpture, aptly named 'Spine' (see p.36 right).

Also in this southern part of the garden are various rusted screens – copies of those used originally in the International Garden Festival in Canada. Kate sold some of the 28 screens, but about half ended up in her garden. As she explains, "You can see them out through the laundry, which is nice, and also they screen our next-door neighbours. When the neighbours have their kitchen light on, it creates a lovely lighting effect behind the screens in our garden, so if we have a party, I ask them to turn their lights on, because we do not have a lot of garden lighting."

The metal gate leading to the studio is another example of Kate's sculptural artistry, and of experimentation – one of the aims in creating this garden. Kate had been interested in microscopic patterning for many years; her favourite thing at university was looking down a microscope. Twenty years later, when she needed a gate, she thought of using this patterning. There are actually two gates in the garden: in the first one Kate made, she felt some of the holes were a little too big, so she made them smaller for a second gate. "It is wonderful to be able to play around with ideas at home", Kate says.

She used a similar idea for a private garden in Adelaide. Here she made a gate based on a postcard (bought in a museum) of a microscopic image of liver cells. She recalls that "the client was going on lots of cleansing diets, so I thought I would do her a cleansing gate! She also loved bling, so we painted the gate gold: it is a bling cleansing gate. I don't know if I ever told her that story! She also loved hot pink, so I used quite a lot of that colour in the plants in her garden, and we added a commissioned sculpture made of Astro Turf. I would like a picture of her all dressed up (she is quite a lovely lady) with a big pair of shears, as though she is pruning it, because a lot of her friends think it is real."

The idea of using red sand is another instance of a past interest of Kate's resulting in experimentation. The first time she used it was as an installation for an arts festival. Then Taylor Cullity Lethlean, with Paul Thompson, decided to use red sand in the Australian Garden at the Royal Botanic Gardens, Melbourne, but that project was put on hold for a number of years. So in the meantime, 'Desert Space' was made in Kate's garden, and red sand or crushed red brick has also featured in designs in a number of the company's other projects, such as the landscape designed around the Uluru Kata Tjuta Cultural Centre. It is a uniquely Australian colour: the colour of the Outback.

The Red Sand Garden in the Australian Garden is now created and is spectacular (see pp.32-3 and 40). It is the first area you see when you walk through the visitor centre, and seems vast, playing with false perspective in that the discs get smaller as they recede from view. Many Australian landscapes are extremely old geological forms, on very impoverished soil, and are highly fragile. The Red Sand Garden mirrors the idea, looking robust, though actually it is not, which ties in with the fact that visitors see, rather than enter, this elusive landscape. A sense of mystery, distance and grandeur is created. As Kate says, "We think red sand conveys a number of things: it enhances a sense of spaciousness; it is a really dramatic

In the garden for a house in College Park, Adelaide, gold-coloured, laser-cut steel screens offer tempting glimpses of the garden beyond.

OPPOSITE: This gate, another of Kate's pieces in her own garden, is doubled in its effect by the shadows thrown onto the ground.

sculptural backdrop; and the colour is very strong and evocative of dry desert landscapes in Australia. We love red or orange sand."

Nevertheless, Kate is, in fact, about to change her front garden ('Desert Space') for the third time. Originally this garden was 'Encircling the Square' – a less stunning space where a square lawn was encircled by fractured stone. Now Kate, who welcomes evolution in her garden, is going to replace 'Desert Space' with ornamental planting, gravel and trees. Significantly, one reason for the change is that Kate and Kevin are thinking of moving, and feel that 'Desert Space' might be too idiosyncratic for the average house-buyer. The new space will also be modern, but more traditional, and not dissimilar from a garden designed for a private residence in Adelaide, but will have some additional dry-stone walling. Kate is interested in combining dry stone (a traditional material) with mild steel (which is modern), and with a contemporary form being in dialogue with the older house.

Kate's garden both gives to, and borrows from, her commissioned work, and this merging of new and old is something she has explored in the gardens of some clients' turn-of-the-century stone dwellings. In these, she has used gravel and clipped hedges, which relate to more historic gardens, but (as in 'Snake in the Grass') are contemporary in their expression. In the one which will inspire her new space, beds of herbaceous plants (recalling Victorian gardens) are edged in mild steel, while the central area (traditionally grass) is filled with gravel and planted in a geometric design. Kate says, "My study of art history has been really important in enabling me to see how the past can inform the present and how there are so many different ways of considering notions of beauty. It enabled me to understand the nexus between art history and landscape history. We often work with contemporary artists as well as historians on our projects."

When asked what it was like being married to a landscape architect, Kate replied, "I find it reassuring; it makes life less scary." She does more of the planting in their work, whereas Kevin is good at running big projects. They are both interested in conceptual work, but Kevin, says Kate, "has a fantastic ability to look at Australian landscape and history, as well as site history. The three of us, Perry, Kevin and I, all have different skills. But out of the three of us, I am the gardener." Kate loves repetition, rather than having too many types of plants, and although she likes flowers, she is really drawn to different greens, leaf textures and shapes. She is also interested in exploring new plants and is particularly keen on Mediterranean perennials at present.

Kate and Kevin do not have a permanent gardener. Kate does quite a lot herself and gets people in to help on an ad hoc basis. Luckily, Kate says, the garden is very forgiving, because she and Kevin travel a lot and it is sometimes neglected. But unlike many designers' gardens, this one is relatively low-maintenance. Kate and Kevin work long hours, and when in Adelaide, find it a treat to drive for ten minutes and come home to a house completely surrounded by gardens. Kate loves being at home with friends and family. She enjoys domesticity and doing housework, and she finds looking at, and being in a garden, really rejuvenating. As she explains, "When we are at home,

with views into and through the garden, it creates a mood of reverie and dream."

From the kitchen, there are café-style doors that open completely onto the north-facing 'Woven Walls', which catches the winter sun. Every evening, Kate watches the light from here. From the kitchen one can also see 'Twisted Limbs', where the bluey-grey-green colours provide a misty quality. The garden is integral to the house in that you can see it from every window. Kate finds that being around a garden really affects her mood, to the extent that while she is making or altering a space and it is just a dirt pile, she would rather not look at it and puts blinds down.

Being in a garden, Kate believes (like Shunmyo Masuno), produces calm, which is incredibly important for everyone, especially young people. Her company has done the landscape design for several universities, providing a release from the concentration of lecture theatres. "You can see students sprawling and sleeping and relaxing and talking," she says, and continues: "I was brought up in Western Australia, where the university campus is quite magical, with wonderful areas, like a sunken garden, and a fabulous courtyard full of peacocks. There was also an auditorium planted with Norfolk pine and you could sit in deck chairs in the evening listening to performances. It was a really formative landscape for me, because until I was six, I lived round the corner and we went there all the time."

Another important influence was Kings Park, an indigenous patch of land with a number of native gardens within it. One of the features of TCL's work is their creative use of native plants (such as cycads, banksias, eucalyptus and angophora) en masse, rather than naturalistically. More recently, Kate acknowledges the influence of the American designer, Topher Delaney, whom Kate admires for her sense of space and materials, and she is also very interested in Japanese gardens. Like them, Kate's garden aims to create a tension between order and informality. Her feeling that gardens have great potency is expressed when she says, "I can imagine what it would be like to live in an apartment and look out at a view. But I can't imagine what it would be like to live in a house that didn't have a garden. If I walked out to paving and bare fences, I would find it soul-destroying. I am extremely affected by what is visually around me. I am a view junkie."

Kate and Kevin have created a garden that is highly designed, and makes visitors gasp, but for Kate it is very personal. As she explains, "Our garden is a really important part of how Kevin

A colleague, who is a performance and visual artist, made a temporary installation in 'Still Water' in Kate's garden. Little squares cut from ornamental grapevine leaves, growing nearby at the time (autumn), are topped with stones.

OPPOSITE: In grey, 'Twisted Limbs', slanting *Eucalyptus leucoxylon* trunks grow from a sea of tufted, arching blue-gey *Festuca glauca*. A sculptural bench made of bedsprings sits beneath a mature apple tree.

and I are. This is our retreat, from which we go out into the world. We do work that it is highly public, on projects that are very demanding, so our own garden is a really important part of us and our relationship. I think being at home, within a garden, is something essential. Each time I come home and open the gate, at the same time as thinking, 'Oh, I should do that', or 'I could have done this better', the overall feeling is of an oasis where you can be in your own world. The garden creates home."

JIM **FOGARTY**

To Europeans, Australia is upside down: its night is our day; Christmas is in summer; and their exotic plants are our natives. Yet although many Australian private gardens might have different priorities, such as pools and BBQs, the general principles of landscape design, including structure, texture, colour, scale, balance, contrast, rhythm and focus are universal.

Jim Fogarty Design is a practice that serves residential and commercial clients in Australia and overseas. His work ranges from small outdoor rooms to large estates as well as show gardens. His attention to detail, combined with his extensive knowledge of plants, has established him as one of Australia's top garden designers and has won him numerous international awards.

Jim has always liked the outdoors. When he left school he spent a couple of years in the infantry of the army reserves (the equivalent of the territorial army), spending a lot of time in the Australian Bush. A friend was going to study horticulture and Jim decided to join him. Fogarty graduated from Burnley Horticultural College in 1992 and gained early experience as a labourer, doing garden maintenance and construction.

Moving from Cairns to Sydney in 1996, he worked on 'Monday to Friday' on Channel 10, presenting weekly gardening segments. Then in 1997 he returned to Melbourne and set up his own garden design business. He now lives in a residential suburb, southeast of Melbourne, with his wife and two small daughters. The street is a post-war development with a mix of '50s, '60s and very modern houses. Architect Paul Delaney designed Jim's house in 2005. The property is not completely screened from neighbours, and benefits in front from looking onto a park with a creek.

The garden, which encircles the house, makes up for what it lacks in size (450 square metres including the house) by what it achieves in impact. Everything has been carefully thought through so that as you wander, you are faced with new and exciting sensations. It is a garden that stands out from the crowd, with its clean lines, grids and strong axes blending seamlessly with the house, which has striking angles and is made of dark ash, concrete and large plate glass windows. In the day the garden is an oasis of calm; in the evening it is transformed into a remarkable space resembling a nightclub.

OPPOSITE: The geometric lines of the house are repeated in the paving but softened with textured planting, with an emphasis on foliage.

ABOVE RIGHT: Wall sculpture and pool take on a new life at night. Innovative lighting by Light on Landscape transforms subdued colours, creating an outdoor entertainment area fit for any event.

MIDDLE RIGHT: The dramatic night-lit shower resembles a mike on stage at a club.

RIGHT: The garage is a hub of vibrant red. Blue light illumintates the double-chiselled lava stone under the bar.

PREVIOUS SPREAD: Detail from p.53.

When Jim bought the property it was brand new, with no garden, providing him with a blank canvas. However, there was a council requirement to keep non-penetrable surfaces to 65% of land cover, including the house. Jim decided to keep the colour of the limited hard landscaping simple and minimal, using white, grey and charcoal as a foil to the planting. Further interest is added in alternating pavers of aggregate and recycled glass. And since the house is double storey, the paving, rather like a parterre, was laid to look good from above.

Along the length of the back of the house is a swimming pool with a dramatic wall sculpture by Valissa Butterworth, its wavy lines in white fiberglass, representing the beach at low tide. Significantly, Jim was inspired to use a similar sculpture by the same artist in his 2011 Chelsea show garden, where it was symbolic of the Outback. Beside Jim's pool, in the courtyard garden, a square of hand-split, bluestone cobbles is used to embellish the paving. Jim felt this courtyard too small for entertaining so ingeniously incorporated the garage space at the back of the house. He changed the white fluorescent tube lights to red ones (for about Australian $20), and in doing so, transformed the garage into a glowing, submarine-like space at

night, complete with PVC and copper pipes of the various services that provide the inner workings of the house.

Many small residential gardens in Australia do not have a great deal of planting, but the required minimum 35% of the space here, which had to be garden beds, mulched area or lawn, was not a problem for Jim. He was able to indulge his love of varied and interesting plants, incorporating them even in the driveway. But the main area of planting is in front, adorning the entrance to the house. Here a mix of ebullient shrubs, flowers, ground covers and grasses provide lush texture and colour. Perhaps surprisingly, there are hardly any Australian native plants: instead they are what Jim calls exotic.

Jim concedes that the notion of an Australian garden is still a very new concept and that many Melbourne gardens have mainly European plants. He explains that "people are a bit blasé about our native plants. It is more exciting to have a European garden in suburban areas." He particularly likes irises, bergenia, salvia, euphorbia, heuchera and festuca. In addition, perhaps because of his recent work in Singapore and Japan, he also loves bamboo. "A lot of people here are very scared of bamboo", Jim says, "so the only chance you probably get to use it is in your own garden. I have used a clumping bamboo and a black one, which aren't as vigorous as common bamboo." A few years after Jim moved to this house, there was a severe drought and he lost some of the planting, but despite this he has assembled a highly luxuriant, discerning assortment of plants. As he points out, "I tend to use more plants than a lot of other people in Australia. I enjoy a contemporary look with a lot of planting to soften it."

Jim goes on to say that most clients would insist on some form of outdoor eating space, whether it be a whole kitchen outside or a BBQ with outdoor table and chairs. He does not have these but there is an informal bar area cleverly tucked between the pool and garage. He continues, "Clients may also be adamant on having a clothesline! If my garden had been for a client, there would have been more of the boring practicalities of outdoor areas that can sometimes aesthetically ruin a garden. We have a portable outdoor clothesline that we put away. For us, the look of the garden is the priority and we work around the practicalities."

LEFT: This courtyard could be almost prison-like, but varied paving, planting and seductive bean bags lend informality.

OPPOSITE: Precise placement, planting and choice of materials contribute to the success of this garden. Flat-leaved bergenia, swords of iris, and statuesque but supple bamboo add another dimension.

Not wanting a small patch of lawn to mow in front of the house, and not allowed more paving, Jim devised a black-stained floating timber deck to sit majestically amongst the dense foliage. This area is primarily an aesthetic one. Two timber 'slats', by Sydney furniture designer, Jo Philippsohn, provide seating from which the garden can be contemplated in seclusion from the street. Since the use of mains water is not allowed, a harvesting tank sits hidden under this area for irrigation.

The garden is used by Jim's family for entertaining and relaxing: his two young daughters love the pool. His wife enjoys letting him do his own thing in the garden and reaping the rewards. Jim does all the maintenance himself, though he says he can go for three months without doing anything and then spend two days tidying it up. On average it requires a couple of hours a fortnight; surprisingly low maintenance. But Jim explains simply, "I like the fact that other people know that I have my own garden and look after it myself so I am not all talk. I think working in your own garden keeps you grounded; you don't become aloof, or lose touch with plants. You still get in there and prune and weed. And it is very relaxing."

So Jim's home garden provides a useful link to his main focus, which is designing gardens for private clients. One such was for a single-storey, Victorian house in Armadale, outside Melbourne,

where, in 2006, he was commissioned to design a drought-tolerant garden. To reduce cost, the existing second-hand, red brick paving at the front of the traditional house was retained, but Jim replaced the dead front lawn with a sea of grasses. Movement, tactility and low maintenance were achieved to wonderful effect. The back garden was decked and screened, making a feature of the impressive peppercorn tree that dominates this space.

A very different garden is one Jim designed in Flinders, Adelaide. Here he took advantage of a very modern house in a fabulous sloping setting, to design an infinity pool as the main feature. The lagoon-like, dream pool overlooks magnificent views across the West Head to Seal Rocks. It is 15 metres long and 2 metres deep, making it an ideal substitute for beach swimming, but it is also beautiful, with sweeping lines, natural finish and an understated grandeur that blends with its surroundings. A cypress deck and shade house inspired by bathing boxes provide the perfect place from which to admire the views.

As well as residential projects, Jim enjoys exhibiting at shows, believing them to be avenues for learning. He has won gold medals at Melbourne, Chelsea, Singapore and Japan. As he says:

"The camaraderie is great; getting to know other designers from other countries; seeing how they do things and learning from other people, whether it be something good or bad that they do. It is easy to be quite parochial and insular and doing shows is a way of expanding your outlook – I find it inspiring."

Interestingly, his garden for Chelsea 2011, 'The Australian Garden', was sponsored by the Royal Botanic Gardens, Melbourne and inspired by Taylor Cullity Lethlean's magnificent, 25-hectare

OPPOSITE ABOVE: In this drought-tolerant garden, Fogarty used South American succulents, New Zealand carex grasses, as well as Australian natives, such as westringia and *Lomandra* 'Seascape'. Soft mounds, tussocks and spikes in a simple palette of greens and browns complement the architecture.

OPPOSITE BELOW: Who would not be tempted to spend all day here? This exquisitely executed pool is in Flinders. Planting is native and coastal, in keeping with the indigenous surroundings.

ABOVE: Fogarty's 'Australian Garden', on Chelsea Press Day, 2011. As well as the glamorous model (provided by the sponsors) the garden includes (on the left) a sand-dune wall sculpture by Valissa Butterworth (who made the sculpture beside Jim's home pool); a pebble path representing a dry river bed; a water feature in the shape of a hunting boomerang; and entirely Australian native planting.

'Australian Garden' (see p.32-3). Jim was commissioned to create a show garden that conveyed a similar concept in a very small space. It told the story of the metaphorical journey of water from Australia's arid Outback, eastward to rivers and gorges, to the urbanised east coast. It included sculptures by Edwina Kearney and Mark Stoner, as an interpretation of their *Ephemeral Lake* sculpture at the Royal Botanical Gardens, Melbourne (RBG) and Jim also only featured Australian native plants, reflecting the RBG's aim to promote Australian planting worldwide. Amongst the plants were several that can be grown in Britain, such as grevillea, with its green, needle-like leaves and crimson spidery flowers, and the silver cushions of *Chrysocephalum apiculatum*, with golden, button flowers.

Two other show gardens stand out in my mind. 'One Country' was Jim's exhibit for the inaugural Singapore Garden Festival in 2006. It highlighted contemporary Australian design whilst showing the diversity and influences of the country. The cascading water feature represented oceans and rivers; forests were depicted in the boundary walls. The central feature was a round entertainment room. Comfortable, curved benches, covered in bright Australian fabric, surrounded a tiered, circular, sculptural light inspired by the banksia flower, with its green core and bands of orange and black stamens.

Jim's design for the Gardening World Cup, near Nagasaki, 2011, symbolised bushfires and the devastating impact they have. Australians love the Bush and many go there to connect with nature, but it is a volatile environment. Hot summers are conducive to destructive fires that can wipe out local communities as well as forests. Yet out of the destruction comes regeneration and new life. Australian plants have adapted to bushfires and in fact many need

them. Heat explodes woody seedpods releasing the contents, and smoke aids germination for the seeds to grow. In this show garden, fire and peace combine. Low, snaking orange walls reflect the colour of fire and the way that the wind can change its direction in the Bush; a small shade structure provides a place for contemplation; water adds a cooling element. Tension and hope converge.

Jim tells me that another thing he likes about shows is that, as with his own garden, they enable you to do things that you probably would not do for a client. You can take more risks or design something that is a bit more 'outside the box'. His clients often want to play it safe and he is reigned in by practicalities. Shows offer new opportunities, which would not even be possible in his own plot. With Jim's home garden, he says that every year he tends to want to start again and do something different, so in some ways it is frustrating. Sometimes he thinks it would be great to do an Australian native garden, but he now has a block of land down by the beach, and he hopes to achieve that there, over the next five or ten years.

Jim concludes: "The fun of having your own garden is that you can do whatever you want. But if you are passionate about plants you always want to change and have new ones every week, which isn't realistic. It is also great teaching my two little girls about gardens and how much fun they are. Seeing kids interact with gardens really inspires me, whether it is herbs or flowers or seeing birds. Just simple things like the sound of wind blowing through bamboo that babies really pick up on." Jim has designed a garden that appeals to all the senses, fulfills all the principles of landscape design, gives him pleasure and inspiration, and delights family and friends both by day and night.

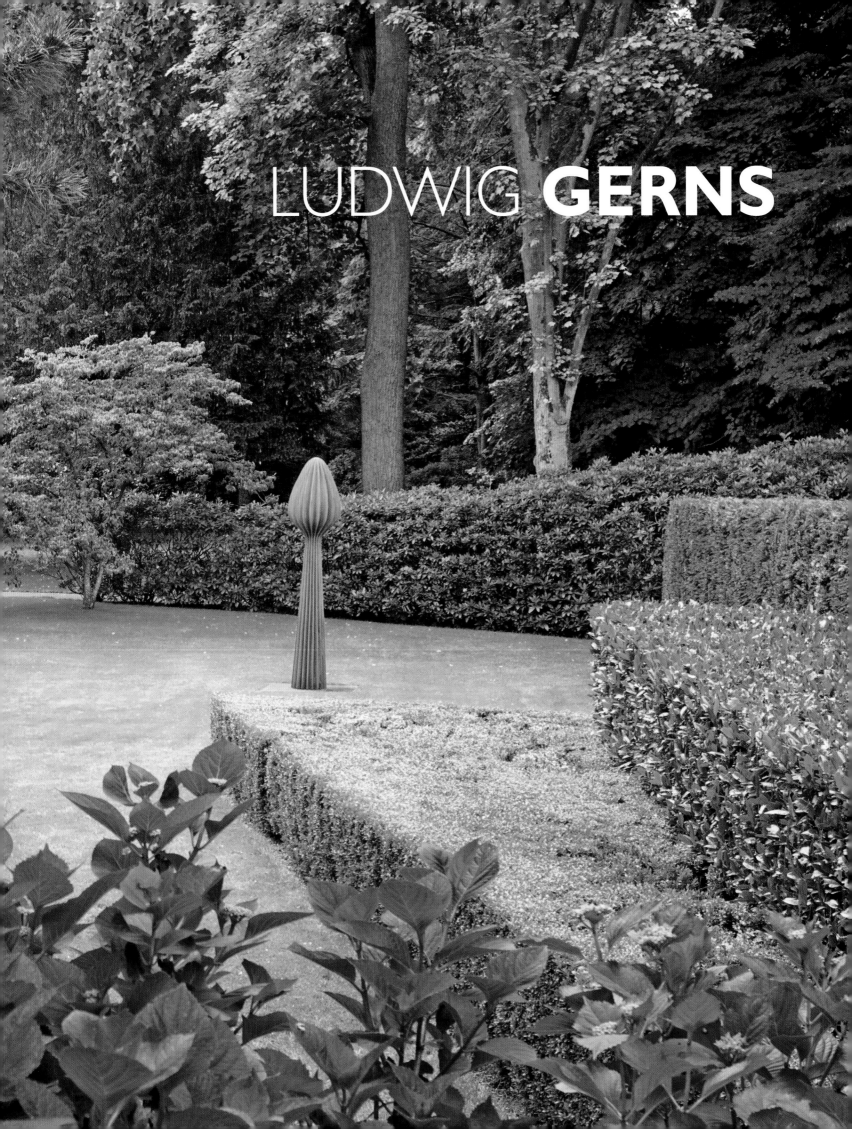

LUDWIG **GERNS**

PREVIOUS SPREAD: Though hedges provide separation, the feeling is not of enclosure but rather of airy spaciousness. The sculpture by Herbert Mehler provides focus.

LEFT: Precision topiary, reminiscent of an aerofoil, greets you as you approach the house. Everything in the garden is meticulously crafted.

BELOW LEFT: The interior of Gerns' remarkable house is a wonderful combination of old and new, just like the garden seen from all the windows. At first the government were concerned about his changes to the listed building; now they are delighted.

OPPOSITE: A view from the fist floor balcony of the house. Squares of santolina mimic the paving. A rhythmic pattern of angles and crescents, with touches of asymmetry, enlivens the classic design.

Ludwig Gerns lives and works in a beautiful house with a glorious garden in the suburbs of Hanover. Texture, attention to detail, idiosyncratic geometry, integrity and tranquility are words that come to mind when describing his landscape designs, though they do not do them justice. But his own garden, even more than his commissioned work, is a place of understated complexity.

The nineteenth-century villa is neo-classical in style and situated on the edge of a huge wooded public park that extends into the city, but also forms the backdrop to Ludwig's garden. He moved here in 1988 because he loved the property and, importantly, could see the potential for making a beautiful garden. He spent over two years restoring the house and garden, candidly painting the older parts of the outside of the building grey and the newer white. The interior is largely decorated and furnished with striking modernity: a very successful contrast to the exterior. It is these two aspects of the classic and the contemporary that are also seen in his garden.

The garden (0.5 hectare) surrounding the house was very overgrown, so Ludwig cleared the area and planted hedges and trees; he also built a pond and cascade and laid wonderfully dynamic curved and straight paths. The layout could be said to be formal, and is sharply defined, but there is also a lively theme of asymmetry running throughout the garden. Planting is mainly non-floral, with temporary flashes of colour (from rhododendron, cherry, azalea, iris and hemoracallis, for instance) in specific places and in calculated progression, creating changing focal points.

Ludwig discloses that for him, this restricted palette is enough, although some clients prefer more colour. Seeing his garden, one can only agree with his views. Especially since the lack of flowers is more than made up for by a great diversity of

contemporary hard landscaping materials: pink and neutral limestone, polished black granite, glass, concrete, stainless and Corten steel, cobbles and gravel. All are used with enormous skill and dexterity to provide not only texture, but balance, contrast and movement within the garden. Moreover, each area flows into the next and has framed views, or glimpses of another scene, so that one's interest never wanes.

Ludwig believes it is very important to have different rooms in the garden. From what is now the back of the house, a central axis runs over sweeping steps to a formal rectangular pond, fed with a cascade edged in stainless steel. To the sides of the steps is a checkered yew parterre filled with santolina; it used to be box, but last year it succumbed to blight. The effect appears classical and symmetrical, except that two trees are deliberately planted asymmetrically either side of the pond, which is actually fractionally longer on one side than the other side at the back. Lines of box hedges border this far side of the pond, where azaleas also grow, pink in May.

To the side of the house, glimpsed through a gap in a hedge and reached by a curving path, is a more open expanse of lawn bounded by precisely clipped yew and box hedges in different formations – Ludwig claims to have invented the technique of flat-cutting expanses of box and uses this in his garden to great effect. On the grass stands a biomorphic sculpture by Herbert Mehler, made of folded Corten steel. From steps next to a side door of the house is a spectacular path, which instead of following the axis of the steps, runs at a 45-degree angle to them. This idea, counteracting the orthogonal (intersecting or lying at right-angles) classical Beaux-Arts style, is unique to the twentieth and twenty-first centuries. It was pioneered by landscape architects, such as the American Garrett Eckbo (1910–2000), who were strongly influenced by Cubism and Art Deco.

For his diagonal path, Gerns has used long, triangular shapes of milled pink limestone, concrete and granite. It cuts through the lawn with a sculptural, modern skew, adding mystery and surprise. Towards the back of the garden on this side, lime and

tulip trees, on site when Ludwig bought the property, merge with the surrounding wood, which appears to be part of the garden.

Walking on through mounded and jagged topiary, one is enticed further round the house. Here, crossed axes are formed by a cloud-pruned yew, emerging out of geometric box, beside steps of polished and natural granite. To the right is the entrance to the house if you arrive by car: Ludwig claims he likes 'driving through the garden'. A straight drive bordered by clipped box and yew, edged with a line of prunus then runs under a wisteria-clad pergola and leads to a garage. Ivy, bound in a ribbon of stainless steel in the shape of a tree, adorns the brick wall at the back of the garden, while in front, a table and chairs are flanked by more differently shaped topiary. Once again, there are framed views towards the carefully placed sculptural focal point on the lawn. Throughout this garden, wherever you turn, you are captivated by a new aspect, as well as different shapes of leaves and surfaces of hard landscaping.

The many landscaping materials run contrary to usual design principals, which tend to prescribe the use of only a few in one garden. But here they blend and harmonise, whilst forming the bones of the garden. At the entrance to the house (which has been changed to be at the back because the government did not want an entrance through the wooded parkland) is a wall constructed of etched glass panels, running the length of the property. The government wanted people to be able to see the house and garden because it is a listed building. Although one cannot really see through, the government agreed to this serendipitous solution.

Ludwig has been solving garden design challenges for a long time. In fact, he first wanted to be an interior designer, but his parents discouraged him, saying he would not make money doing this. He became interested in gardening when he was about sixteen, and a couple of years later, a friend of his father, who was a garden designer, advised him that first he should study practical horticulture. This he did, as well as later going to

the University of Hanover, to study theory. His parents paid for this as a way for him to later earn his own money. First he tried to get work in the United States, because he was interested in their gardens, but he did not find a job. So he returned to Germany and got his first client, shortly followed by more, and was able to start his own practice. He recalls that a long time ago he wanted to design golf courses, but found that there was too much beaurocracy involved. Now he designs largely in Germany, Austria, Switzerland and Majorca, about 80 per cent of his work being for fortunate, private clients.

Clients naturally want to incorporate their own ideas into their gardens. Ludwig takes these ideas and combines them with his own, so building long-lasting relationships. He feels collaboration is important in order for the client to feel that the garden is their own. Nevertheless, Ludwig says, "I have my style, and you will find it in all my gardens. I often work with hedges to make rooms and prefer not to see the garden all at once, but perhaps in teasing, small views. If you live in the country and have vistas and landscape, then it is different, but for small city gardens, this is not a possibility and clipped evergreens, with perhaps a path

running into them, mask limits. And hedges define spaces. The use of buxus is not new – it has been used for centuries – but I have taken the idea and made it modern. As in a house, you need different rooms with different atmospheres. In my own garden there are changes from graphic to modern to more formal in several places. I think it works better with the house, which I feel is extremely important."

The atmosphere is one of tranquility, and Ludwig uses the garden to relax, but does not have time to be in it a great deal. He also sometimes uses the garden to test certain plants, assessing how they grow and flower and what colour combinations work – something very important to him. For example, he dislikes yellow with red, but enjoys harmonious affiliations. So trial plants will, occasionally, be taken out. Ludwig employs a couple of gardeners, two to three days a week, increasing the number twice a year when the hedges need to be cut. He also finds the garden useful as a way of displaying his style to clients, whom, he explains, often find it hard to understand his concepts from just words, plans and models. When he shows them his own garden, clients understand. Sometimes, they say, "I would like something just

like yours", but Ludwig says, "No, I never do the same thing twice. I can use the style, but not the exact detail." Clients have also come with a picture in a magazine saying, "We want this here, and that there." Then he will say, "OK... But what do you need me for?" As Ludwig explains, "Each garden must fit the client and the property." In fact, Ludwig will often go inside the client's house to explore the ambiance that makes them comfortable, as inspiration for their garden.

"Each garden designer has his own ideas," Ludwig continues, "but I can only do what I feel. Sometimes clients ask for something that is not my style or my feeling and I tell them I cannot do it. The chemistry has to work. The best clients say they have some ideas and then let me do the design. Then we discuss it further, and after that I can start and it will be a good garden."

One such, which Ludwig took me to see, was an incredible private garden in Hanover, near his own. The owner has travelled a lot and wanted this reflected in the garden, with the

Flowing, sensual and sharp lines are typical of Gerns' work, as is the detailing of the stainless steel edge to the water in this immaculate garden for a house near his own.

OPPOSITE: In Gern's client's Japanese garden, shaped topiary enfolds the space, while a mirror (reflecting the maple) decoratively appears to double the garden's size.

result that there is a French lavender garden; a delightful Japanese garden (complete with an original tea house sourced by Gerns from Japan, which took five months to reconstruct in Germany); an Italian garden; a pool that might have come out of a Hockney painting; and statuary (the owner has an original Dalí). Every plant and stone is placed with care. Stainless steel is used to edge a gravel garden, gold to pebble a stream.

Money was clearly no object for this client and the 0.8-hectare garden is intensely and immaculately maintained by three gardeners every day. The owner told Ludwig he wanted a beach, so Gerns created a pond sloping up to a small sandy

shore complete with deck chair. Every wish was granted. Each area has its own theme and atmosphere and again, the predominant colour is green and texture plays an important role. The garden, like the house, is modern and opulent, accentuating all of Gerns' design gifts, though I actually preferred the greater restraint and subtlety of his own garden.

Not all Gerns' commissions are on such a lavish scale, but they are nonetheless impressive. One example is his design for another dramatic garden in Hanover, where house and garden converge; a second is a scintillating garden in Hamburg, on a hillside near the harbour. Here, all the elements used – water, steel, a landing stage – reflect the harbour figuratively. Most striking is a wooden catwalk, typical of Gerns, dissecting the garden at a diagonal. At its end is a view of the large ships coming into port. This garden also has a restricted colour palette, and strong horizontal lines, adding an illusion of size. As

with Ludwig's own garden, it is architectural and exhilarating as well as intimate and personal. And like all his gardens, including his own, it has similarities with the twenty-year-old Mercedes Benz sports car that Ludwig drives: it has quality workmanship as well as style and beauty. But unlike his car, the design details of his gardens are cutting-edge twenty-first century.

OPPOSITE: For this garden in Hamburg, a typically dynamic design is achieved using a limited colour palette and vertical, diagonal and horizontal lines are offset by foliage.

BELOW: In a private garden in Hanover, a screen with a cut-out square hides the extended terrace from the entrance of the house. Fabulous topiary, and chairs designed by Philippe Starck complete the picture.

ADRIAAN GEUZE

Although Adriaan Geuze is a founder member of West 8 Urban Design and Landscape Architecture, based in Rotterdam, where he lives and works, his own garden is in Catalonia in northern Spain. Since 2008, this has been where Adriaan comes with his family to relax.

Like Adriaan and all his work, his garden fascinates. Though homely and peaceful, it is also filled with energy, excitement and innovation. And while this garden is small and private, it has nevertheless been a testing ground for future public projects. Built on a hillside, Geuze's garden has three levels, each of which is 4.5 metres higher than the next. Every level has a different character and each is fabulous in its own way.

The highest garden is a striking enclosed space surrounded by three concrete walls (a typical material used by Geuze). One is solid and, as the garden matures, will be entirely covered with ivy, vines and climbing plants. The other two walls are constructed from open hexagonal shapes, looking like giant concrete honeycombs. The cells will be filled with stones that

Adriaan gathers from the forest – a lifetime's occupation; at present the walls are about a quarter filled. He takes any stones that he finds which are not too small and that he is able to carry, and fills the spaces in the wall with different patterns.

On the fourth side of this area is a small patio, where the family sits in summer. "Lunch is a serious business in Spain", says

OPPOSITE: Though the design for this part of the garden came about as an experiment for a large public project, it is completely personal here, where Adriaan is slowly filling each honeycomb with stones he finds.

BELOW LEFT: The stones are arranged in an intricate mosaic; each hexagon is individual.

BELOW RIGHT: Shadows of the unfinished wall form a reversed powerful pattern on the grass.

PREVIOUS SPREAD: A fabulous, flowing footbridge, containing a wooden bench, spans the linear VSB garden in Utrecht. Long, low box hedges, lines of red sandstone chippings and large sandstone blocks contrast with the discreet bank building.

Adriaan, "and the place we have lunch and drink wine is a kind of wind tunnel, so there is a pleasant breeze." From the patio one can see the garden through a gate made of metal hexagons. The house, which sits between the top and middle terrace, is largely built of white plaster, and this, too, Adriaan intends to completely cover in climbing plants: "I think it will take ten years," he says, "although the eastern side, outside the kitchen, which gets the morning sun, is already cloaked in wisteria. But after only three years, it does not flower. We talk to it every day, and will wait another two or three years and then the bombardment will start." On this side of the house, too, on the highest terrace, is a kitchen garden, where the family has breakfast.

Perhaps unexpectedly, Geuze claims, "I am a landscape architect steeped in tradition". He explains that he decided to invest in good soil, irrigation and basic structure first. Another priority was to create a link between the upper and the middle garden, which he did by forming a slope covered in rosemary and lavender. These flower between spring and August, providing pollen for the bees that live in a hive here. The kitchen garden is filled with herbs and vegetables conducive to growing in this mild corner of the Mediterranean. Last year Adriaan and his wife added flowers in pots, as she loves blooms and colours. This area is not really planned, but as Adriaan concedes, "The more the better. It is a little bit extravagant."

The middle terrace creates another change in tempo; it is formed of a grove of twelve irregularly planted mulberry trees, pruned to create a horizontal roof. Half the trees were bought when twenty years old, and half were three years old, but the green canopy is now complete, only three years after planting. In this shady green glade hammocks are slung between the branches of the trees, creating a magical space. The three bedrooms in the house, side by side, have sliding windows and small wooden terraces that look out onto this garden and beyond, to the Mediterranean sea. First thing in the morning you can walk straight out onto this more linear terrace, which is approximately 6 metres wide and 40 metres long. The garden is parallel to the road and perpendicular to the house.

The mulberry garden plunges straight to the bottom terrace, which is forest. This was here originally, but much got demolished before Adriaan bought the plot, during the construction of the house, so he has replanted it. There is a natural spring, but it is hard to find, as the trees are so thick that

Suspended elegance and tranquility define this space.

OPPOSITE: The Mediterranean sea, glimpsed throughout the terraced garden, is framed by the hexagonal wall.

one can hardly walk through the forest. Looking to the left, far off is the Mediterranean. The house is south facing over the valley and Adriaan and his wife bought it because they loved the view. Now, additionally, throughout the year, Adriaan finds joy in the garden.

This is how he describes it: "In winter this garden provides a kind of Zen therapy when I prune the mulberry trees, and in summer I love to carry stones to the garden and, with a little mortar, I add them to the hexagon structure. This garden exists to reorganise my brain!" He goes on to comment, "We dramatically over-use the garden. We have a dog and children; there are always family around and we build tents, or sit in the sun.

The upper garden is very windy, but by building walls and enclosure, we have created a microclimate, which is fantastic. Actually, some people do not like wind, but I love it. Then in summer, if it is too hot, we have the mulberry garden for shade."

Adriaan believes that his personal garden is part of how he functions when at ease. "For instance," he enthuses, "life here consists of half an hour of picking and ritual exercise in the herb garden, resulting in drinking mint tea and eating your own salads. It is lovely. Of course we are not always here, but then our neighbour takes the produce, so it is not wasted. It is simple but important. But pruning in winter and filling the wall in summer is magic. I love it." Whilst in Spain, he and the family also go to the beach and for walks, but Adriaan reckons that every second day will be spent in the garden.

When designing for clients, Adriaan tries to find out their character, what they will do in the garden and what it represents for them. He calls this discovering the narrative or storyline. Then he decides the structure, trees, hedges, soil and water. Lastly there are details – mosaic paving, for example – and then comes the ornamental planting. This method does not really change. But his own garden, Adriaan claims, is not a design object, but his home space.

As he points out, "I know many landscape architects who make their own gardens wonderful, as showcases for what they can do. But for me, it is not the case. The hexagon may look spectacular, but it is there by chance, first because we needed enclosure and secondly because I wanted to check it out for something similar on a much larger scale in the Maxima Park in Utrecht. Like the doctor ignoring the health of his children, but saving the lives of others, it is the same with my own garden." The children climb trees and play football; his dog undermines the slopes. He would like to trial artichokes to eat, but he does not get to do this because his wife likes the flowers. This garden is, he says, not typical of his work, although like many of his other projects, it is a place of fun.

The design for Maxima Leidsche Rijn Park, west of Utrecht, is not yet completed so this is an artist's impression. Along one of the edges, shielding the park from its suburban surroundings, will be a huge pergola of honeycomb design.

OPPOSITE: April 2011 saw an amazing installation of red bridges above a sea of swaying bamboo as the centerpiece of the Xi'an International Horticultural Exhibition in China.

Though Adriaan designs gardens and parks for clients, as the director of West 8, founded in 1987 (when he was 27), he is predominantly involved with large-scale urban planning and design. After winning the prestigious Prix-de-Rome in 1990, West 8 (named for the strong wind that sweeps across the polders of the Netherlands) established a reputation on an international level, with its successful technique of relating contemporary culture, urban identity, architecture and public space in ecologically responsive designs.

Geuze's projects (like those of Ron Lutsko, Jr.) spring from an interpretation of the emotional needs of city dwellers. He creates challenging, conceptual landscapes grounded in Dutch tradition. They are often whimsical and poetic but also exciting, eye-catching and dramatic. They are characterised by artistic flair and originality combined with functionality. He has a penchant for strong lines, water, bridges, the colour red, playfulness and wit. West 8 has won numerous awards and design competitions, such as Toronto's New Central Waterfront concept in Canada; a 35-hectare park on Governor's Island in New York, which, interestingly, will include a hammock grove; and Maxima Leidsche Rijn Park, Utrecht, which will feature a four-kilometre long pergola, formed of irregular hexagons.

This wall of hexagons, when built, will be on columns 3 metres high. Adriaan wanted to see the effect of the concrete shapes

and decide on the thickness of the wall, so making a small prototype in his family garden was very useful, and showing photos to the clients helped to convince them. Geuze explains: "If you are a landscape architect sitting in an office, now and again you hesitate. So I thought, 'Give it a chance. Let's see how it looks.'" Since Adriaan only works with local craftsmen, this was quite a complicated task. There was no precedent for building a wall of hexagons that was both robust and elegant. He eventually found a local welder who made small hexagonal moulds that could be reused to build the concrete structure. This enabled Adriaan to envisage the scale required for Maxima Park.

Another garden which was brave in concept was that made for an exhibition in Xi'an, China, in 2011. Adriaan's brief was to make an installation to be visited by a lot of people, yet that required only a short time to build. This went against his belief that gardens should take a few years to create. For Xi'an, an ancient Chinese city, he came up with the idea of building a garden of 10,000 bridges. That was the narrative. It arose from part of the Tao philosophy, which embraces the theory that life has many obstacles, but by overcoming these you become wiser. Some typical elements from Chinese landscape painting and design were used to create an illusion. Geuze asserts, "That is what gardens do; they can do nothing more. A garden has no function – just like poetry or music. No one really knows what gardens are for, which is what makes them so special. They are places to dream and to be otherworldly."

The result was a small plot with a winding, labyrinthine, narrow path through tall, dense bamboo, and five hump-backed, scarlet bridges, which allude to the 10,000. The bridges are positioned in such a way that when you are in the garden it is completely unclear where you are, how many bridges there are, or what number you have walked over. The path loops over itself so that you go both under and over the bridges. There is one bridge that is higher, giving you a view over the landscape, and this is the only place where you can grasp a little of the reality. Adriaan says, "People come out smiling and excited. And because the bridges are wonderfully curved, they have a relationship with Chinese history. So the garden is a Western reflection on Chinese culture, shapes, colours and metaphors. It plays with your memory. It is both familiar and new and people have to colonise it themselves – and that is what I believe a garden is."

Adriaan's own memories are of a childhood spent in the Dutch countryside. His father told him, "The landscape is yours," and taught him how to jump over ditches with a stick and to hunt, with the result that as a young boy, Adriaan and his cousin were always far off, about 20 miles from home. This was totally normal for him. His garden was the Dutch landscape: the dikes, the meadows, the cows, the horizon. And this had a huge influence on his work.

Adriaan explains: "The logic of Dutch landscape is very artificial. You say that my work [like a garden made of pinecones for a monastery in Italy or an installation of three inflated, eight-metre-high cows along the highway in Randstad] is surreal, but maybe it is just that I am Dutch, and the whole country is artificial. We live on the reclaimed seabed. All European cultures have a different perception of nature. The English have a very romantic idea of gentle rolling landscape, given by God. In England there is also the tradition of the rural garden, with citizens coming from the country and trying to keep a little of the spirit of their agricultural background alive in their gardens. The Dutch, on the other hand, believe that they can build nature. They think they can create a new nature."

In one of Geuze's designs, however, he used nature, seemingly untouched. 'The Swamp Garden', which I loved, and which he believes was perhaps his best, was created as an installation for the Spoleto Art Festival in Charleston, USA, in 1997 (see pp.72-3). This demonstrates his love of landscape, but this time, instead of creating something artificial within it, he actually captured, or netted, a part of the surroundings to make a stunning garden, although for Adriaan, it is the narrative which is important.

Sometimes, Adriaan admits, you do not have a specific sentiment about a site. This happened at Charleston, so he drove into the country to get inspiration. Charleston was one of the ports where slaves were brought into the United States; the countryside was thought to be good for rice culture, but this did not work, so people abandoned the plantations and nature took over. Now the area is full of cypress trees, swathed in Spanish moss, with crocodiles, mosquitoes and turtles in the swamps. The shallow water is black, forming a perfect mirror. This is what

Adriaan saw and he decided to change the site for his installation. He picked a place he found from a small boat. It could only be reached by walking through the swamp over a twisted boardwalk, at the end of which was a deck and a bench formed from a dead cypress tree, found on site, sawn in half.

A rectangular structure of four steel poles, interconnected by steel wires, hung with Spanish moss, created an open-air room. In the breeze, the moss was in constant motion, like hair. Adriaan describes how "you could sit there, sweating, because it was very humid, and imagine that any moment a monster from the swamp could appear. It created an amazing, bizarre experience, at once relaxing and frightening. You could literally cry because it was so confronting. This garden was really good, but in the second year the wires rusted and broke and the garden was gone."

Seating is an important part of Geuze's designs. He points it out in his own garden, and in his design for the new headquarters of Verenigde Spaar Bank (VSB) in Utrecht, it is extraordinary (see pp.64-5). Geuze linked the building with the surrounding ecological park with an exuberant, 200-metre, steel bridge, which has a bench along its length. As Adriaan says, "That is of course very surreal because it makes you sit, or uncomfortably, not sit. Some of it is sloped so you will slide down! This garden is beside a skyscraper where people sit at a computer all day endlessly dealing with numbers. They break out at lunchtime, so I made a garden with flowers and box hedges and a bench where they can sit in the sun. I like the questions: 'Is it a bridge or is it a garden or is it a bench?' I believe that it is important that gardens are not too simple but that they encourage new and exciting experiences. This is the child in me. I feel that designers of gardens and public spaces should provide elements that people can discover, whether physically or mentally. Children always inhabit everything they see personally, even if to adults it appears dangerous. They do not see a difference between a playground and a car park."

Gueze's designs are site-generated (inspired by and relating to the setting), contextual (using the conditions of the location) and postmodernist (a reaction against spare, minimalist Modernism – full of cultural references). This could be said about his own garden too, but that is also the story of his family. His wife is an actress, and he says, "She is completely differently wired than I am. I am an engineer; she is always looking at people and thinking, 'What makes them tick? Why do they do that?' She does this every day to the cats, the dogs, the children, everyone. But she is also intuitive and when she buys a plant we put it in the garden immediately with no concept." When they find something on the beach it is put in the garden; when Adriaan's wife sees a tree she likes, she easily persuades him to buy it. Things happen haphazardly: it was actually a water ban in Spain that made Adriaan look for drought-resistant rosemary and lavender.

Adriaan says, "Normally, when I design, I think about the project for weeks in order to come up with a narrative and then I will do everything to make that into a garden: there is complete control. My own garden is different. It is for a happy family to fool around in – and it works!" Adriaan's childhood, playing on the artificial, man-altered landscape of dikes and polders, has left its mark, for Geuze's gardens have the mystery and surprise of surreal artifacts. His garden in Spain bears these traits too, especially in the parts that are, unusually, prototypes for other projects. But it is a wonderful family garden painted with his brush; Adriaan's own garden is his private way of life.

THIS SPREAD: 'The Swamp Garden' (for a festival in America) is only about 11 metres x 9 metres, though it encompasses a vast, spectral scene. Curtains of Spanish moss form a box, fencing in and delineating nature. In the morning the beard-like moss is pink in the low sun; in the evening it is white. Water lilies, silence, the sun's rays and reflections, as well as alligators, inhabit this magical place, which, like a story, also holds the thrill of possible danger.

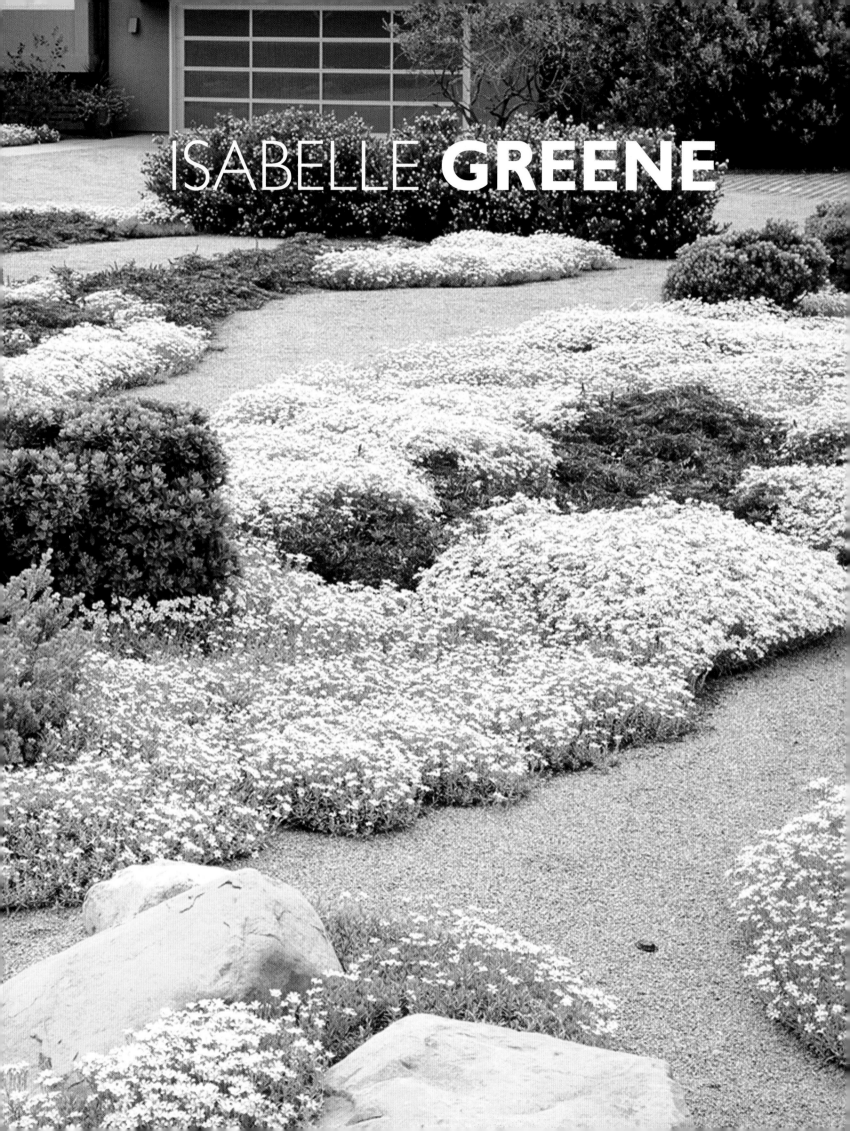

ISABELLE GREENE

There is a special pleasure you sometimes get when speaking to someone you admire, with whom you sense a certain rapport, and who is generous in sharing their experiences and thoughts. I was lucky to feel this when I had the chance to talk with Isabelle Greene about her garden.

Isabelle combines the wisdom of age with infectious impishness. She was born in 1934 and is still working at the firm she founded in Santa Barbara, California – Isabelle Greene & Associates, Inc. – except that, as she jokingly puts it, "I've cut down on my business hours. I've cut all the way down to full time." Her ground-breaking and award-winning gardens range from modest to extensive and they pioneered a new aesthetic in Santa Barbara, where European pergolas, lawns and axial paths had previously been the aspiration for many garden designs.

Isabelle has a regionally specific approach, and uses native plants that are drought-tolerant. Her designs incorporate their surround-

ings (both natural and man-made); she is enchanted by the landscape, and its abstracted images echo through her work. She is also strongly committed to sustainability. Isabelle works in the tradition of Ed Bye (1919–2001, an influential American designer who wrote *Art into Landscape, Landscape into Art*), allowing the land to speak rather than imposing the designer's ego onto it. A sense of spirituality runs through her work, but she also has an evident playfulness and liking for whimsy. Additionally, Isabelle pays great heed to the wishes of her clients, involving them deeply in her work. Her gardens are personal and evoke strong emotional responses; she has likened them to memories, strewn within the landscape.

Her most famous is the 'Valentine Garden' in Montecito, which she designed in collaboration with the owner. It is located on a steep slope and was created in a time of drought. A stream of slate, scattered with agaves, anigozanthus and yuccas, intersects terraces inspired by rice paddies in Indonesia and farmland in America. It is as if a vast landscape with rivers and lakes has been seen from a

LEFT: Isabelle was asked to create a silver garden within the glass house of Longwood. The sensual slate path was inspired by her walks in the deserts of California, where flash floods cause tracery in the sand, and Isabelle's walkway imitates the wash.

RIGHT: Greene's masterly use of texture and knowledge of silver-foliaged plants, adapted to dry climates around the world, shines here in the 'Silver Garden'.

PREVIOUS SPREAD AND BELOW: In front of this stark, modern, client's house, a foam of sparkling white *Cerastium tomentosum* fingers the gravel.

plane above (Isabelle enjoys flying over the country, seeing patterns in the landscape and taking photos) and reduced in scale to make a piece of art, which is this iconic garden. It led to many more commissions, including the fabulous 'Silver Garden' at Longwood Gardens, Pennsylvania.

Another client's garden that I love belongs to a beach house that is situated on a strand between the Pacific Ocean and a marsh, where rivulets of water come and go. The garden reflects both aspects with brilliant planting. On the ocean side (behind the house, see p.78) the planting is restrained, rugged and green. The configuration of the slew in front interested Isabelle: sometimes there would be slick bodies of water inter-fingering amongst the marsh plants; at other times it would be mud. She recapitulated this patterning in front of the house, which is only separated from the marsh by a small road. Groundcover of white-flowered *Cerastium tomentosum* in gravel beds seems to be formed by the ebb and flow of the marsh tides.

Isabelle's own garden is considerably smaller (only 0.3 hectare) and is perhaps less innovative, but it is equally beautiful and, like its owner, possesses immense personal charm. Isabelle describes her garden as eclectic, saying, "I am a person who never thinks in boxes. I love to fly off in new directions. Every garden is a journey and experiment and challenge, including my own." She has lived here since 2005. Most of the lot faces south and it has heavy clay soil, which Isabelle has come to like. It retains water, is rich and, although you cannot dig it, if you put mulch on and let the worms do their work, she finds it is a blessing.

For Isabelle, though, it was less a matter of choosing a garden than considering the house, garden and setting as a whole (as she would for a client), because to her they are one. First, she carefully selected the neighbourhood. She describes it as, "A two-block long street that doesn't go much of anywhere so it is quiet with little traffic. It is a neighbourhood dating from the '20s and '40s, so it is stable and a little bit quaint. Many houses were built by returning servicemen, so they are modest but each house has individuality, and I like that. My house was a 1948 mail-order house. It came in parts, with ludicrously simple instructions, and was assembled on the lot."

Another advantage for Isabelle was that the north views (in front of the house) are of mountains. She saw that there was a small house across the street that didn't obscure the mountains at all, and this was very important to her since she loves their majestic presence in western California. Additionally, the generous southern aspect sloped, and she knew that there would be a chance to have deep views there and make a garden. The house Isabelle recalls, however, "was terrible". It had no eves, just "a dumpy red roof that came right down to the walls, the way a child draws a house. It had a red door in the middle and

OPPOSITE: This dramatic use of sparse planting for a beach house seems in direct contrast to Isabelle's own garden. But as always, the design is sustainable and not only reflects, but echoes its setting. The mound-like shrubs, *Pittosporum crassifolium* 'Nana', that tolerate salty conditions, appear as though self-seeded in the wind.

ABOVE: A curving path descends through terraces. Sensitivity to texture is evident again, with swords of iris leaves mingling with feathery Queen Anne's lace, beneath the apricot tree Isabelle saved when she bought this plot.

and a ficus about to uproot the foundations. There was also a conifer planted very near to one of the apricot trees and the two of them were fighting it out. The conifer took light from the apricot so it leaned away "in a kind of ballet-like stance. Having to choose between the two of them, I removed the conifer".

Not too many changes are made in the garden now, for Isabelle says, "My life and my head are so full. But occasionally something will die, and I am just delighted that I have got a space for something new!" Working in her business and running a household, Isabelle does not have time to do all her own gardening any more and has gardeners. "I do all the pruning and grooming and training and deadheading and cutting, but they do everything else", Isabelle tells me. I could not think that there *was* much else, but she continues, "When I go through the garden and trim, I leave heaps of stuff behind me."

The design for the garden did have an overall plan, but each part had to be thought through separately, which is the way Isabelle designs all gardens. She decided that, as she was already in her seventies with a couple of bad knees, and her husband is older than her, thinking ahead, she wanted to be able to wheelchair in and out of the front door, if necessary, on a flat path. Beside this she has planted a blend of eight or nine different, ground-hugging plants of the same height, with similar foliage and texture. Isabelle explains, "Since the neighbourhood is quite traditional, I thought we should have something flat and green there. I think it rather funny that my husband still refers to our front lawn."

Behind the house the lot slopes down, so Isabelle decided to build the garden on a series of flowing terraces; she tends to find geometric lines dull. Since conservation is important to her, the concrete footings that were knocked out from the old house, which was improperly built, were broken up and used to make the terraces. You step out of the bedroom onto an old irregular stone slab, then walk about 4.6 metres at the same level, but then the ground drops away. Isabelle, typically, accommodated what she had, having fun in the process. As she delightfully phrased it, "I am very used to designing magnificent gardens for other people: they must look right, suit them, serve their social needs and status needs. For my home garden, I was almost like a rascal, mischievously knowing that I didn't have to do any of that. This is for me and my husband." In fact, Isabelle remarried after she had bought the plot, but before she moved in, so it started out as a house and garden for her but became a place that is shared.

Isabelle's garden is serene (like her commissioned work), and she says, "I abhor busyness", but it has a cottagey feel, all the more impressive because it belies the artistry and organisation

windows on each side and it had sunk six and a half inches in one corner, and one of the rooms had a floor that was completely termite-ridden and the whole house was ugly inside."

The house was and still is 102 square metres. This space had eight or nine rooms in it, but when Isabelle went to view the property she immediately envisaged eliminating all the walls. She now uses the space almost entirely as one large room. Her second thought (typically) was that when you come to the front door, and enter, you should look right through the house to a garden. The details of how to rearrange the house took over a year. Isabelle measured everything, such as how much space you need when you pull a chair out from a table; if you are sitting by the fire, how close you have to be in order to keep warm; how wide the area for walking round something should be – all these details took time to consider. But then the house developed. Now, when you open the door, you are in a big room with lots of windows and French doors through which you look out to the garden.

If you go round a corner of the room to the L-shaped back portion of the house, you reach the bedroom. This faces the garden too. Isabelle explains, "I wanted to be able to wake up in the middle of a garden." So here, too, two walls are made up of floor-to-ceiling French windows (reminiscent of the little house where Isabelle grew up, in Pasadena, which had a screened-in porch). Now Isabelle and her husband's bed faces straight onto the back garden.

When she arrived, the lot was almost bare except for self-seeded hollyhocks, an orange tree, two very old apricot trees, a loquat

The charming vegetable garden is seen through a multi-stemmed loquat tree.

OPPOSITE: Arching over the fence is Rosa 'Madamme Pierre Oger', a Bourbon rose with slender stems bearing scented, creamy pink, double, cupped flowers. When Isabelle talks of this, it is as if she is recalling a dear friend. "I adore that rose", she says.

that has created this space. There are picket fences, stepping-stones, a round kitchen garden, fruit trees, no lawn, dense colourful planting on the terraces, and a comfortable air. Isabelle describes it as "a household garden". The vegetables blend into ornamental flowers because refreshingly, Isabelle admits, "I have an aversion to this fad about garden rooms." Her whole garden has a coherence and 'oneness', possibly a throwback to growing up in Pasadena in the '30s and '40s, when people tended to have a front lawn with a hedge and a gravel drive, with a backyard filled with glorious spring grasses that died in the summer, leaving a bare plot with a fence dividing it from the neighbour's backyard.

Isabelle determined that she did not want to fill the entire area with planting. She managed to get a 'vacant lot' feel at the back, by planting it with a few shrubs but leaving space for spring grasses to grow. She is also a keen composter, and campaigner for sustainability. As she says, "I have a love for this Western land that I grew up in and have hiked all over. And my degree is in botany so I understand life processes, and know that we are running out of everything: oil and water and air." She also believes that using native plants is exceedingly important and works hard to urge their use with her clients. Her argument is that any desire can be met by using native plants. In her own garden some natives, such as *Prunus ilicifolia* (Catalina cherry), *Heteromeles arbutifolia* (toyon) and

Ribes sanguineum (red flowering currant) are used specifically for the berries they produce for birds. She also has some unabashed favourites, such as the shrub spiraea, which was in her grandfather's garden; ceonothus, with its powdery, deep blue flowers and evergreen foliage; and *Viburnum plicatum* (Japanese snowball bush) that is traditionally grown in the eastern United States.

But apart from providing pure pleasure, Isabelle's garden is also a working experimental garden. The cost of it comes out of her business and she tries out plants, especially new species and exotics, to see if they will work out the way she specifies when designing for clients. Because of her curiosity to see how something will grow, her planting in her garden is often in ones and twos, which she says is "a no-no in design". However, Isabelle rightly claims that the discipline she imposes here means that the plants blend into large masses of colour and height and horticulture.

When Isabelle sees a new plant in the nursery that she wants to experiment with, it has to go into a section of the garden, if there is space, where the ecology is going to be compatible. She has dry and moist, sunny and shady, low and high areas. She also considers the height before deciding which terrace to plant it in. Thought is given to the colour of the foliage – whether grey, silver or green – as well as the texture of leaves and whether or not they are deciduous. Finally, the colour of the bloom has to fit into her complex scheme, which is partly determined by the colours inside the house, for Isabelle shares the Japanese gardening ethos of interior and exterior merging into one.

The bedroom walls are a dusky grey mauve. Isabelle knew that she didn't want the colour orange to fight against this. So the colour scheme of flowers in the garden, including pond plants, marginals and everything else, beginning at the left of the bedroom, starts with white and goes through yellow; then blue to purple to pink opposite the bedroom doors. To the right of the pink and the path, is pink and red combined into cerise; then there is true red, and around the corner there is red/orange. Out of site from the bedroom there is straight orange and to the far right is yellow. Everything has to fit into this highly organised pattern. Admittedly, this sort of colour

LEFT: This espaliered apple tree originally grew in a small copper planter outside Isabelle's condominium. She trained it there for about ten years, and when she moved, placed it under a stained glass window in her house, planting *Aeonium urbicum* (succulents) beneath, which she likes to mix in with 'normal' planting.

OPPOSITE: The man-made pond looks entirely natural with white *Iris japonica* on the far bank spilling into the water. It adds a soothing element to the garden as well as encouraging wildlife.

scheming is not unusual in long borders, but it is extraordinary in a whole garden, and it is even more unique because it derives from the colour inside the house.

Despite this seemingly regimented approach, the garden appears quite natural. Isabelle deliberately aimed to make it joyful, enclosing and restful for her and her husband: in this she has skillfully succeeded. Previously, Isabelle lived in a condominium, with no neighbourly feeling, too much cement and hardly any garden. However there were raccoons, which she occasionally saw at night, and a possum. This made her want a little wet area for wildlife in her new garden, which would be viewable from the bedroom at night.

Now she has a nostalgic, naturalistic-looking pond on the upper level, overlooked from both the bedroom and kitchen. Isabelle originally wanted a little moist and muddy place, but that would not work on clay soil (which heaves when it is moistened), so it is a rubber-lined pond, with re-circulating water. It is approximately 4.6 metres long, more of a watercourse than a pond, reminiscent of a tarn in the sierra. The edges are dexterously disguised with large stones and ground cover planting such as creeping thymes and potentilla as well as with irises.

There are a lot of glorious irises in Isabelle's garden, because actually, the planting has evolved partly through chance. When Isabelle moved in there was a little patch of maroon and mauve irises in the front, under a pine tree, which were not thriving. She transplanted them from the shade to the sun at the back, and then someone gave her some blue irises, which she added to the garden. As she admits, "At first you are just looking for ways to cover up the ground."

Other changes have arisen through self-seeding. Isabelle says she did not realise that Queen Anne's lace (*Daucus carota*), seeded so profusely. It is not as widespread in California as in Britain, and Isabelle remembered it as a magical storybook plant, with its delicate umbels of tiny white flowers. She had seen it flowering in the fields in Oregon and as a child in Virginia, and one day found a pack of six small plants in her local nursery. There was a little space at the edge of the irises next to some eriogonum, so she planted them. They grew up much taller than Isabelle expected, to a height of about 2 metres, and she says that it was glorious to see the effect they had on the lower terrace and how much she and her husband enjoyed looking at them from the bedroom. Then they got spindly, so she staked them; as they matured and went to seed, they were interesting too, and so Isabelle left them. She admits she also lets lettuce, chard and parsnips go to seed because they are beautiful. Next spring the Queen Anne's lace sprouted up all over the garden, and she left quite a few of them, where the colour worked.

A similar thing happened when Isabelle bought some opium poppies. After they had flowered she saw the wonderful, fat oval of the seed heads topped with a matching green ruff collar at the top. She wasn't going to destroy these, so she left them till they got brown, dry and hard, when she harvested them to use in dried flower arrangements. In the meantime she took them into the garage, and while waiting to hang them up, she laid them on their sides. Then Isabelle recalls, "You know how garage projects are. About six months later I noticed the garage floor was quite gritty and dirty so I swept it out the side door. But it was actually blackened with poppy seeds. So the next spring, outside, all through the strawberry patch, hundreds of poppies sprung up. We let them grow, and there was a poppy forest fully five feet high [1.5 metres] of all colours of poppies, and the strawberries withered away and we couldn't get into the side door of the garage anymore, but is was so much fun." Now the poppies are banished to the back of the lot, where Isabelle is experimenting with a wild flower area.

These fortuitous 'accidents' are less likely to happen in clients' gardens, nor would one find experimental planting. In other ways, however, Isabelle's garden is more similar to those of her commissions than many designers'. This is because she designs in very different styles according to her clients' wishes (including colourful and cottagey), as well as the soil and the situation. She feels that in some ways the process she uses to create any garden is the same – answering various needs, but always making something coherent. She also believes that the workings of nature, unadulterated, are extremely interesting and that it is more rewarding to let go, and see what happens than to impose your will on everything and make it go a certain way, "which is rather grim". Isabelle hopes that her clients' gardens, like her own, will be for fun. Significantly, she says, "I try to get them child-like and in the mode, if I can."

As a child, Isabelle always looked at things carefully. She still remembers when she was two, sitting on a clover patch in the grass on a summer day, enthralled by the rounded shape and the smell of the clump of clover. When she was four or five, she already knew how she would like to see things be and would make mental readjustments. As she grew up she was always constructing models out of cardboard and clay, eager to try to put things together in the nicest way and rearrange what was actually there. Painting was another part of this, as was her first notion of becoming a studio artist. Now Isabelle does not have much time to draw, but she consoles herself saying, "My medium is the world. I sculpt with giant rocks of 50 tons and with groups of men and huge machinery. I feel good (listen to this!) that I am transforming the world in a better way." Isabelle is not being immodest. There is no doubt that garden design, especially at her level, is an art form of significance.

I feel that Isabelle Greene and Dan Pearson share a certain amount in common. Both have a deep sense of the spirit of a place and create site-generated designs; they believe gardens can intensify physical and mental alertness; and both are still influenced by their childhood. In Dan's book *Home Ground*, he writes, 'I have gardened since I was five or six and feel lucky to have found that passion so young and I completely equate to the theory that the activity you loved doing most as a child – the state of utter absorption, is the very thing you should find a way of repeating as an adult.'

Isabelle says, "I think I am kind of childlike and part of me never quite grew up. I love sitting in my gardens. I love to go

This ingenious, stunning design is Isabelle's driveway. Hating hard paving and solid cement, and not wanting to lose garden space, she devised this enviable solution. She poured some cement wheel strips, adding pink pieces of broken concrete from other sources, and then planted a variety of different thymes between.

back to them, and not be required to improve, or comment, but just to sit and let the happenings happen – the birds and the sunshine – it is like sitting in that clover patch. I think that is my greatest joy, since I am such an intense person and so busy, to let my brain loose. I almost inevitably experience euphoria."

BUNNY **GUINNESS**

Bunny Guinness is best known in Britain as a regular panellist on BBC's *Gardeners' Question Time*, as well as for her writing and her gold-winning show gardens. After graduating with a BSc in horticulture, she went on to qualify as a landscape architect, setting up her own practice in 1986. But Bunny is unusual amongst other designers of her calibre in that she designs largely alone, rather than heading a team, and she provides a unique, approachable service to clients.

In addition to full design specifications, Bunny offers a one-day consultation (for a fixed fee viewable on her website) where she will help a client understand their garden and its potential and come up with solutions to design problems on the spot, providing a sketched master plan shortly afterwards. This means her commissions vary from tiny city plots on a tight budget, to extravagant gardens complementing substantial properties for the likes of Sir Bob Geldof and Crown Prince Sultan bin Abdul Aziz in Arabia, to shopping precincts in Europe and a public park in Japan.

The key to the popularity of her designs is that they are practical as well as gracious, and appeal to adults and children. Her attention to detail and imaginative hard-landscaping elevate her work to the exceptional, while she also combines romantic sensibilities with expert plant knowledge. All these qualities are evident in Bunny's own, sublime garden near Peterborough, in Cambridgeshire.

This country garden is divided into eight distinct areas that surround a beautiful, L-shaped house, parts of which date from the thirteenth century. Bunny bought it in 1987, largely because it was in the cheapest area with proximity to London, where her husband was at that time working. When I visited, 25 years later, in autumn, beds were not packed with rare specimens as in a plantsman's garden, but structure and repetition were prominent, and the whole seemed much larger than its 0.2 hectares. This measurement does not include the woodland,

ABOVE: Cloches from Bunny's 2011 Chelsea show garden now nestle in her personal plot.

LEFT: Yew hedges frame the voluptuous kitchen garden, where double cordon apple trees, like giant forks, emerge from lettuces.

PREVIOUS SPREAD: Pink cosmos and sedum, textured foliage, grey metal and dripping quince complete this scene in early Autumn light.

which was the first thing that Bunny planted. It took her about a week and a half to plant the 1,000 small native trees (ash, wild cherry, hawthorn – the climatic vegetation), which she did before unpacking and settling into the house.

The plot is on top of a hill, swept by southwesterly winds, and planting the wood totally changed the microclimate, as did the addition of many yew hedges. Before Bunny arrived, the house was a rented farm and there was no garden, just one or two apple trees. The courtyard to the south was composed of concrete, tin shacks and telegraph poles, while to the north, fields came right up to the house. In fact, when Bunny watched television (in a magnificent vaulted crypt), sheep would come up to the windowsill, which is at ground level, and watch it too. The present kitchen used to be tin-roofed sheds but is now the heart of the house, with doors which are normally open leading straight to the garden. As the house developed, so did the garden. The result, whilst filled with artistry, is unpretentious, with an atmosphere of intimacy combined with joyfulness.

In front of the low stone house, clad in wisteria, honeysuckle and *Trachelospermum jasminoides*, is a courtyard. It is paved in squares of stone and thyme, with a central square of shell mosaics shaped like ammonites, on which stand a metal table and chairs. In each corner of the courtyard, quince trees bearing downy, yellow fruit perfume the air. This is the more remarkable since the soil is actually very shallow here. Formal beds, edged in box, contain feathery, annual cosmos and plump sedums in a largely pink

palette of late colour. Each year, however, the planting will change. As Bunny explains, "I wouldn't want it the same every year. I like it to be ephemeral, while the structure remains mainly the same."

Recent additions to these beds are beautifully crafted metal obelisks taken from Bunny's 2011 Chelsea Flower Show garden. She says that she likes to do something new in her garden every year and incorporating these was her project for 2011. There are box balls and 'stone' ones, as well as a bench supported by balls. These look just like stone but are in fact coloured concrete, made by a firm in Cheshire, to match a piece of stone Bunny sent them. They are used throughout the garden, providing subtle visual links. Bunny is a believer in what her husband calls GSTDI (get someone to do it), so for paving, willow work or woodwork she has regular artisans and craftsmen whose skills she uses. A local carpenter has also created all of the gates according to her design.

Through one such, is a passageway that links the house and Bunny's workplace, and leads to a stunningly picturesque, productive vegetable garden. This too, has recently been enhanced by cloches from the 2011 Chelsea garden. Raised beds are filled with all manner of vegetables, including pumpkins, chillies, peppers, potatoes, leeks, chard, cabbage, lettuce and cucumbers, as well as herbs, for Bunny aims to be self-sufficient. There are also decorative terracotta pots containing standard bays and laurels, and candelabra apple and pear trees, grown as double cordons. The colours are largely grey and green and there is a sense of symmetry and order amongst the abundance.

LEFT: The landscaping principles of Henry Tipping, garden designer and writer (1855–1933) were, 'to retain the grace and feeling of the wild, while adding the eclectic beauty of the cultured'. Guinness fulfills these gloriously.

OPPOSITE: One of many hand-crafted gates forms a focal point at the end of the ammonite and stone path, dividing delightful box pens of topiary chickens.

To the right is a terrace by the house, with dining table and cushioned seating overlooking a large lawn. A ha-ha creates a seemingly endless vista into a meadow inhabited by velvety, black cattle and brown sheep. A large ash tree, with a seat around it, heightens this area of green openness and pastoral serenity.

Continuing round, a wonderful willow arch leads to an old orchard and children's garden with a serpentine grass path between ash trees, underplanted with ferns and bluebells, aconites and foxgloves. Here there are two tree houses, one thatched, both immaculately crafted. This garden is not child-friendly in the normal sense that implies compromises have been made to its appearance to accommodate children; it is a wonderland. Perhaps this is not surprising considering Bunny is the author of a book entitled *Family Gardens*. Ambling past a greenhouse, one is surprised by an area equally arresting for adults and children: an enchanting box parterre housing topiary chickens. A path of ammonite mosaic down the middle ends in a customised gate leading to the open countryside beyond.

To the east of the house is a formal, rectangular lily pool in a walled garden. It is surrounded on three sides by avenues of pleached hornbeams, unusually, linked together to form a pergola. At the bottom of one avenue is a mirror, doubling the architectural impact. Beside the house is a border of mixed native and exotic plants. *Erysium* 'Bowles's Mauve' mingles with roses, hydrangeas, poppies, herbaceous clematis, irises, salvias, lilies, euonymous, geraniums, grasses, agapanthus, agave, macleaya, and *Canna iridiflora*. Repeat planting and swathes give cohesion. The atmosphere is comfortable and secluded.

In this garden one slips in and out of formality. On the other side is a wildlife garden in woodland, in which Gloucester Old Spot pigs and chickens roam. The chickens have changed their location various times. Bunny tells me that each batch is different. They used to be in the yard in front, but they kept coming into the kitchen, which is the origin of the pretty wooden gates Bunny has installed. At the moment the chickens roam in the woodland, though two saved from a battery keep coming into the vegetable garden. All of Bunny's livestock are home-slaughtered by a man who comes to the house, avoiding them being taken away under stress.

For the last ten years Bunny has employed a gardener one day a week, but she does most of the work herself. This she enjoys but she also believes that gardening keeps you healthy and fit, and unusually, has written a book on this subject, too. She is genuinely interested in health; her son is studying medicine and her father ran the marathon aged sixty-five, never having run before. Bunny points out that horticulture is not only good for you physically, but also for your mental wellbeing: "Gardening keeps us happy in many ways and that whole area fascinates me. Three hours gentle gardening is equivalent to one hour thrashing away in the gym. More people should do it."

Bunny has used the garden in different ways over the years and her family is woven into its fabric. Her husband (who does not enjoy gardening but whose permission is sought before major changes are made) likes entertaining in the garden and relaxing on the comfy chairs on the terrace. Bunny says, "He makes all the moves in the house, like saying, 'Let's do up the kitchen'. But outside it is me who instigates and does things." The garden has also been a safe and exciting play environment for children, where they not only had tree houses, but also a Wendy house, trampoline, sand pit and paddling pool, as well as wild areas to explore.

Now the garden provides self-sufficiency, with fruit and vegetables as well as Soay sheep and cattle enhancing the view from the kitchen. As Bunny says, "the cattle are friendly, so there is a nice rapport with them and they are also rather like sculpture." Productive and picturesque, the garden is also a place where Bunny says she learns. Explaining that she cannot imagine life without a garden, she asserts, "I don't feel I know a plant until I have grown it. Some people on landscape architecture courses know very little about horticulture, but I love plants, and find design fascinating, so the garden is a place for me to play around in."

In fact she comes from a horticultural family: her uncle is David Austin and her mother owns a nursery and "is batty about plants and a bit of an obsessive". But this made Bunny rather a rebel. As a child, Bunny (so nicknamed at birth because her eyes looked like currants in a bun) got bored with the Latin names of plants. She was paid two and sixpence to weed the drive, which was huge, and a real chore. At that time she was more into horses. Later she did an applied science degree and worried about being in a white coat for the rest of her life. When she met a horticultural student, who told her about working outside, Bunny

Opposite: A new orchard has been planted west of the kitchen garden. Box balls meld in a hedge; box doughnuts encircle fruit trees. Structure and definition are achieved in the squares of uncut grass.

Above Left: A small gap entices the eye. From the kitchen garden you are drawn towards a path bordered by containers of standard laurels.

Above Right: Lead obelisks add height to beds in the courtyard, with Japanese anemones below.

Right: Bunny sits amongst her vegetables, *Erigeron karvinskianus* at her feet.

decided to take a year off, work in horticulture, and then take a degree in that, followed by one in landscape architecture.

Bunny has succeeded triumphantly in a profession which, in England, is dominated at the top by men. There seems to be no clear reason for this. Bunny, however, points out that at Chelsea most of the people on the judging panel are male and she feels this is relevant. In her view they are setting the standards, and often like bold impractical gardens, which are not necessarily what the public likes. She feels that these gardens are design statements, possibly like modern male art. "I think men also tend to be slick at

ABOVE: This wonderful den, formed from a hollow, pollarded willow (previously in Guinness' Chelsea 'Wind in the Willows Garden') now augments a private garden – a typically imaginative idea.

LEFT: When Bunny took Clare Wilks to Hokkaido, they designed this willow nest. There is a little seat inside, overlooking a river. This simply beautiful tree house would not be allowed in a British park due to health and safety regulations.

MAIN PICTURE: A perfect English orchard created for a park in Japan. Low fencing and step-over apples add child-like charm.

business", Bunny continues, "but I don't like employing people and running a huge company. I like working across the board, including planning, construction, engineering, and horticulture. And I enjoy doing *Gardeners' Question Time* and my *Sunday Telegraph* column and being able to pick and choose and do my own thing."

Because *Gardeners' Question Time* is recorded live, Bunny has to think of answers to immensely varied questions on the spot.

These are chosen by the chairman and producer, unseen by the panel. Their range is huge: hiding neighbouring eyesores (try planting pleached trees); how to preserve container plants while on holiday (add a water-storing polymer to the compost); recommended plants to intersperse with paving (*Sagina glabra* or *Thymus serpyllum* 'Minimus'); stopping mint spreading (plant in a container with the bottom removed or an old washing machine drum); the cause of apple leaves with brown wiggly lines and circles on them (they have been attacked by the apple leaf-mining moth, which does not usually cause long-term damage but can be sprayed with insecticide).

Answering questions such as these makes Bunny particularly good at trouble-shooting and dealing with the public. This is reflected in her way of work, which she loves, because she says she is always learning from the people she meets. She explains: "I enjoy the collaborative aspect of going to someone else's garden. I like arriving at a couple's house after they have had a survey and they tell you what they want – often both having different wishes, and you thrash out a solution together and re-jig it till it works." She also advises on sourcing, pointing out that many people still believe they can get everything from a local garden centre.

Bunny has worked in this way for many years, saying that to start with she worried that maybe she would not be able to come up with the goods, but that has never happened. "The more you do, the more strategies you have for dealing with problems of ugly sheds, or seclusion, or improving levels, or whatever the client wants." Restricted colour, Bunny advises, is often a good way to pull a garden together, as is repeat planting. "Lots of people have underground basements now", she continues, "with problems of light and restricted soil depth and getting large things into confined spaces. One luxurious day with the client can either end with a drawn plan or go on to more detail and the normal tender processes."

But Bunny does not always work on small-scale projects. Her largest challenge was a public park in Hokkaido of over 20 hectares. While European parks sometimes incorporate a Japanese garden, here, a quintessentially English garden was the brief, and who better to fulfill that than Bunny Guinness? Enormous quarries, described by Bunny as "looking like the moon landscape, with no vegetation and vertical six-metre wall drops", were transformed into 23 glorious gardens, including an orchard, a maze, grottos, lakes, underground tunnels, a willow dome, tree houses, a sheep farm, a sculpture garden and many more. There is also a rill, looking like a giant staircase going down the quarry, made of ammonites, trialled as paving in Bunny's own garden.

This park in Japan was commissioned as a result of Bunny's Chelsea show gardens. All of these demonstrate her skill, but

her 2011 garden was unusual in being a functional, contemporary vegetable garden. Luxurious combinations of cabbages and roses, beans and clematis, in a scheme of lime-green and wine-red, spilled from curvaceous, raised, woven willow beds. These surrounded a lead dipping pool from which the garden could be watered. A large, 'floating' glass platform at one end provided an elevated space to relax and view the vegetative beauty and pattern of the parterre, as well as forming a protected area below.

One of Bunny's private commissions on a grand scale is Holywell Hall, Lincolnshire, redesigned for the late Prince and Princess Galitzine. Superbly sited, on a broad south-facing slope overlooking an eighteenth-century lake, the gardens include a beautiful formal pond, a wonderful walled kitchen garden and handsome herbaceous borders. This was the second garden Bunny designed for the Princess and so the relationship was strong. She was a medic and Bunny believes that many doctors are great gardeners, though the Princess also had several full-time gardeners to help her.

Bunny claims that all her gardens are different because they reflect her clients' briefs. In contrast to many designers, who say

their own gardens are higher maintenance than ones they design for others, Bunny says that if she had a full-time gardener, she might have more herbaceous borders. Her garden, she asserts, does not look picture perfect, but she would not like lots of staff picking up every fallen leaf. "We all like slobbing out here", she says. This splendidly derogatory statement has one element of truth in it; Bunny's garden feels comfortable. It also has perfect proportion and balance and combines a rural idyll with prettiness, productivity, play areas and personal touches. This garden, which is never open to the public, is neither ostentatious nor fussy; it is very English but not boring; it is enduring – the more you look the more you gain; it is enchanting and truly inspirational. It is the sort of garden that I imagine very many people would love to own.

ABOVE: Guinness epitomised: a palette of just yellow, green and bronze in repeat plantings of ebullient, shade tolerant hemerocallis, *Alchemilla mollis* and cordyline bejewel a south-facing rill at Holywell Hall, Lincolnshire.

OPPOSITE: A dancer, provided for Chelsea Press Day by M&G, the sponsors of Bunny's 2011 garden, poses in the potager. In the foreground are red cabbage, *Lavandula* 'Regal Splendour' and *Knautia macedonica*.

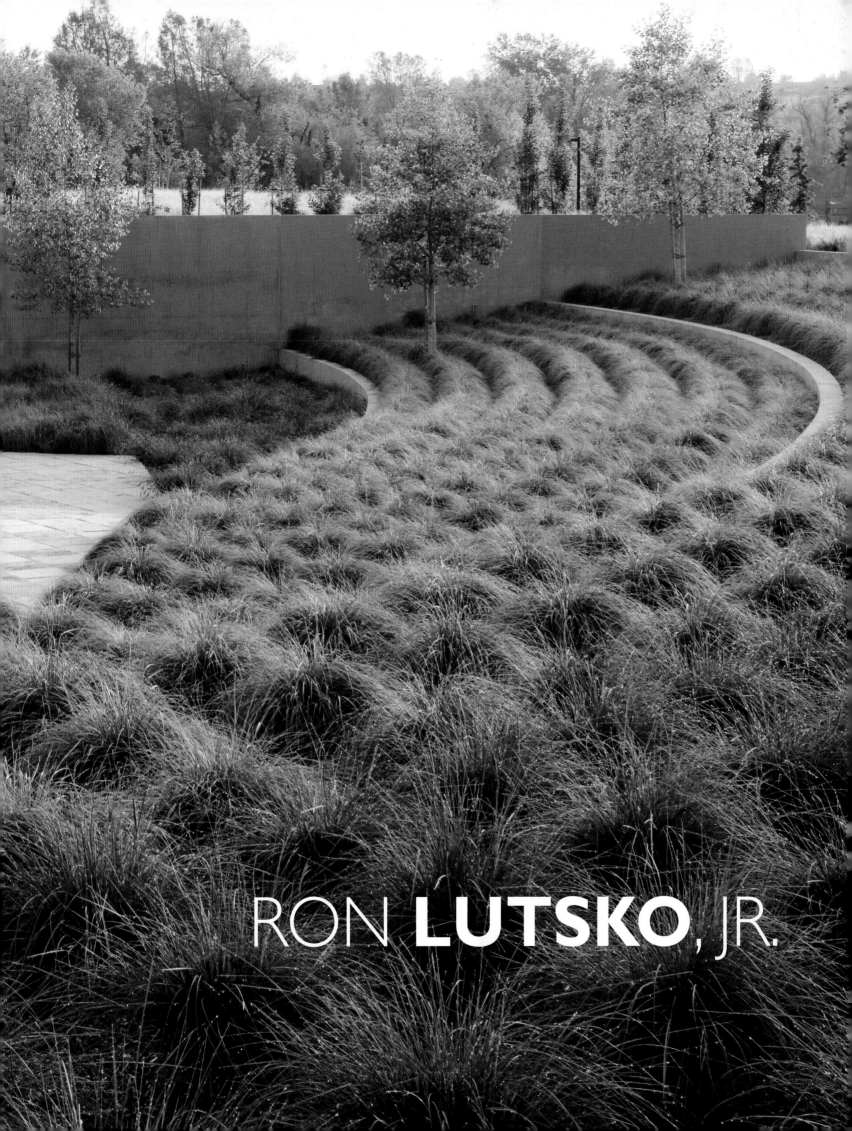

RON **LUTSKO**, JR.

Ron's idea of bliss is being close to nature, particularly in the Capay Valley of California, so it is not surprising that although he has two other houses with gardens (one in the Bay area of San Francisco and one in the mountains), he chose his farm in Guinda to represent his personal plot. It is also the garden he is most actively engaged with now.

All the gardens Ron designs are site-generated: inspired by the geology, history and culture of the locality as much as from information visible to the naked eye. Simple, unifying ideas speak of the surroundings. Ron is also a Modernist, fascinated by man's intervention in nature. Following in the tradition of the eminent American landscape architect, Dan Kiley (1912–2004), Lutsko embraces functional land use and the belief that gardens should reflect the work of man. Like Caruncho, Lutsko delights in lines of vineyards and grids of city streets, incorporating them into his designs.

Formal geometry, classical axial views and pared-down simplicity are important elements in Ron's work, so at first sight, his farm garden appears to be very different. But is it? Certainly it is more indulgent and less precise, but the same spirit presides.

The garden feels expansive, open and uncomplicated. It fits with its surroundings, and as always, ecology is amongst Ron's guiding principles. He, like Perazzi, favours indigenous, and preferably local plants as key components in his designs. Ron is passionate and knowledgeable about his native flora and its preferred growing conditions, and his farm garden, along with his adjoining native plants nursery, fulfills this enthusiasm.

But above all, perhaps, this garden has an endearing lack of pomposity. It is a family space where both of Ron's daughters got married and where capricious elements evolve, become

PREVIOUS SPREAD: A snaking rill in the 'Sustainability Garden' at Turtle Bay is constructed with native materials. An amphitheatre of indigenous deer grass, *Muhlenbergia rigens,* planted in rows, adds texture and contrast.

ABOVE: Ron, his wife Sandi and daughter Sarah, relax in the shade of an oak tree in front of their house.

OPPOSITE: Sandi and Sarah picking vegetables. Bearded iris thrives along the fence, while the water tower (now inoperative) bears the lyrics of a song loved by Erin, Ron's youngest daughter, who wrote it here at the time of her wedding.

part of the place and stay. This is not at odds with the Modernist precept, also held by conceptualists, of the social role of public spaces and gardens. Lutsko is critical of soulless minimalism and, in both his commissioned work and in his farm garden, he seeks to create places that have relevance to people's lives now.

Ron's interest in gardens started as a child. He, along with his brothers and parents, lived in his grandparents' house for five years, when Ron was aged five to ten. He was fascinated by everything in nature and his French grandmother, who loved gardening, encouraged him and let him help her. They would plant marigolds together and tend her rose garden, nurturing his interest in plants.

While his grandmother was a gardener, Ron's mother was fascinated by history, and his father was a scientist – each helped form him. Ron's first degree was in horticulture; his second in landscape architecture. He taught at the University of California at Davis for about ten years and then, surprisingly, took a Masters degree at UC Berkeley, designing his own programme. Significantly, he studied a combination of cultural geography, art and architecture – especially Japanese architecture and gardens – which remains very evident in his work.

Early on, Ron was influenced by a lot of good design, ranging from his studies of the Italian Renaissance to Roberto Burle Marx (1909–1994, a Brazilian landscape architect). He admires gardens such as Sissinghurst, claiming to have the plans of many iconic gardens in his head. Later he became fascinated with contemporary Californian gardens, concluding that they were misfits in their social and regional contexts and disliking the way in which many designers treated plants as static objects. While he was intrigued by their use of materials and their minimal aesthetic, he wanted to break away from what he saw.

Ron founded Lutsko Associates, in San Francisco, in 1981. As its principal, he has worked on residential, commercial, civic and institutional landscape designs throughout the world. The studio is known for creating projects that balance clean lines and intersecting planes, in an interplay of different hard landscaping materials, with flowing, drought-tolerant and native plants. Their work has been at the forefront of sustainable design and is both modern and ecological.

Driving to Capay Valley Farm, a 28-hectare parcel of land north-east of San Francisco, one passes mixed scenery: rocky hills,

The drive to Ron's farm is planted with oaks on one side and olive groves on the other. Pots of euphorbia enhance the verge; rolling hills add majesty behind.

BELOW: Ron keeps chickens on his farm and is nearly self-sufficient. A co-operative of small, sustainable family farms operates in Capay Valley and runs a farm shop.

OPPOSITE: The barn, housing all the farm tools and equipment, is framed by oaks. It is sited directly opposite the house, with the lawn between.

pale soil, native oak trees and cultivated olive groves. Turning west, into a long drive, the terrain is the same but subtly tamed, so that native meadows are augmented with anemone, asphodels and sage. Iris and narcissus line the drive and large, cast-iron metal planters (originally for boiling lard) hold euphorbias and agaves, interspersed between an impressive avenue of native oaks, planted by Ron. As the drive narrows, the planters become smaller, containing succulents, the scenery is less arid and open, and you pass through a shaded wooded area with a stream. Finally you come to a natural clearing in the trees, and passing by an old barn you arrive at the white, wooden farmhouse.

The house was built around 1880, but has two additions of about 1920 and 1950. It is what Ron calls, "classical vernacular without much thought behind it" and he recalls that the whole place was a wreck when he bought it. In fact, the people that determined the value of the house in 2004, when he bought it from the federal government (who took it over after some illicit activity had gone on there), deducted $12,000 from the value of the property, because that is what they thought it would cost to tear the house down! But Ron and his wife, Sandi, fixed it up and made it homey. They bought the plot for the land in order to start a plant nursery, but also inherited olive groves, thus becoming olive farmers as well.

Ron spent the first year cutting down improperly planted large old shrubs and trees and doing a big clean up job. As he explains, "A large part of the beauty of the place was achieved through editing and removal as opposed to active design. Although I did have a master plan, as I would for clients, it was not detailed." Ron considered how the drive should end, where the parking would be, where the beds and paths should be, and he planned the circulation and how the parts would relate to each other. He also had overall ideas of the general planting: not specific species, but where there would be low woodland plants, tall screening plants, rows of trees etc. The rest developed as he went along.

Ron's farm garden, like his commissioned work, is in sympathy with its surroundings, looking as if it belongs to the wider landscape. This is something he feels strongly about, especially, in rural or agricultural settings. Intriguingly he says, "I think this is achieved through a combination of form, textures and the leaf quality of arid plants. To some degree composition plays a part too. Off the top of my head, if you are planting a bed in front of a distant hillside that has a combination of seven different kinds of foliage or colours, you might pull that same combination into the bed in the foreground."

Another of Ron's interests is in modern architecture, with the ideas behind his landscapes being similar to those behind contemporary buildings. Although his farm is old, he admits: "I really have very little interest in looking backwards, when it comes to design. I am far more interested in contemporary issues and trying to address them in the landscape. If someone wants a traditional garden round a French farmhouse, they should talk to someone else." Having said that, Ron continues, "There can, nevertheless, be a kind of correlation between Modernism and simplicity." Ron concedes that the farm garden does not feel as modern as some of his other projects because it is more relaxed and informal. It does, however, reflect man's part in nature, which is a topic that fascinates Lutsko, and which he strives to articulate through his work.

The basic structure of Capay Valley Farm garden is simple and organised, with clearly defined spaces nestled amongst barns, a couple of chicken coops and outbuildings. There is a sense of intimacy in the areas near the house, with their richly textured planting, while views of oaks, olives and mountains provide an omnipresent backdrop. One unusual aspect of the garden in this part of the world is the large lawn, which Ron acknowledges is incongruous from a work and climate point of

view. But the farmhouse came with a large lawn, and although he reshaped it, he did not get rid of it, since a giant, 100-year-old pecan tree shades it all summer.

At the back of the house, Ron created a kitchen garden with fruit trees interplanted with artichoke, fava bean and row crops, bordered by a fence with grapes, berries and bearded irises. This part of the garden is actually as big as the ornamental parts, but these latter are important too. Ron admits to being an obsessive plant collector, and in his other two home gardens, "plants are crammed in helter-skelter fashion". But here, on the farm, he says, "I am trying really hard not to default to that. So although there are a lot of plants here, they are treated a little more thematically with a bit more organisation and repetition. I am trying not to end up with a horticultural mess – but it is hard for me!"

Beds of mimulus, with their colourful, snapdragon-like flowers from spring to autumn surround the parking area. Between this and the house are wide spaces planted with euphorbia, lavender, penstemon, yucca and cardoon, while beds around the lawn hold a multitude of shrubs and perennials. Next to an Airstream guest trailer is an un-irrigated, desert-like garden where mainly silver, strangely textured plants thrive, along with a collection of rosemary: there is aromatic artemesia, rosettes of aloe, spiny opuntia, woolly leucophyta, showy-flowered cistus and pomegranate. Finally, on the banks of the creek, Ron grows phlomis, salvia, grasses, sphaeralcea (a shrub with mallow-like flowers) and epilobium with their racemes of white flowers.

The plants are mixed – not all natives – but they all fit the environment, whether it be because they are drought or heat tolerant. The climate at the farm is closest, in European

terms, to Morocco. Water harvesting is of limited use, because the rainy season is so short that the amount saved is always inadequate for year-round sustainability. The majority of Ron's plot is not irrigated, so he is reliant on his horticultural knowledge of which plants will survive. He does have a well, but his water is high in salt and in boron, which is toxic. As Ron says, "We couldn't grow a magnolia or a dogwood if our life depended on it. After about a month of our water, *Helleborus hybridus* looks like someone had taken a blow torch to it." One of the keys to his success here is growing plants that do not need water so they are not affected by the boron. Many plants from the desert of northern Mexico as well as plants from southern Europe do very well. A handful of plants that one would normally expect to need water succeed too; they include heuchera, Asiatic lilies and fruit trees.

ABOVE LEFT: A river of acid green *Euphorbia ceratocarpa* runs in front of a silver Airstream caravan that serves as a guesthouse. In the foreground are the silver, needle leaves and chartreuse yellow flowers of *Euphorbia* 'Limewall'. The hearts along the fence were for Erin's wedding, but Ron says: "We like them so we will leave them there."

ABOVE RIGHT: Soft grass, grey olives and green oaks. "I shouldn't have made a garden. I should have just left it like this; it is the prettiest place", Ron jokes.

The garden is used to grow a lot of the plants that Ron wants to propagate in his nursery. Chamisa Ridge Nursery primarily services his own projects but is also a commercial enterprise. It is not actively marketed, but anyone who comes along is welcome to buy plants. It is dedicated to growing species suited to arid conditions, with a focus on plants not readily available in the nursery trade. The majority of the plants hail from the American West and can survive without irrigation – new plants are discovered every year.

A pattern of grids – in the door made by Ned Kahn, in shadows on the wooden deck and in reflection in the glass wall – combine to delicious effect. Two quaking aspen trees add nature to the man-made in this private garden in Idaho.

OPPOSITE: The Ketchum garden is both an extension of the house and of the landscape beyond. Airy foliage and blossoms in the foreground acknowledge the wild beauty of the setting. Woodland trees anchor the house in its surroundings; sharp hard landscaping shapes the whole.

Ron reveals: "The garden is actually a giant experimentation site. It is where we grow our parent stock for propagating. It is also, perhaps most importantly, a centre for my family and all our circle of friends to gather and eat, play and have fun. We have an orchard of about 35 trees and a vegetable garden, so we use it for our personal food production too." Ron also makes olive oil for sale. Spanish, Arbequina olives grown on the rich alluvial soil are hand-harvested and pressed within four hours. The oil is renowned for its sweet, grassy flavour.

"This valley is actually an epicentre of organic farms," Ron explains, "so if we don't have something ourselves, another farm will have it; we hardly ever need to go to the store. The neighbouring farmers do a lot of trading. Rather than using money, they often exchange, for example, work or olive oil for lamb. The area works as a very informal cooperative. It is fun."

Ron spends three or four days a week here, saying it means a lot of different things to him. He believes that a garden creates a particular atmosphere that is conducive to intimacy with family and friends. The hard part, he says, is the balance: "If you like gardening, which I do, it is easy to spend less time than you want to with your family and friends." On the whole he manages, because although the vegetable garden requires a lot of work, for example, everybody picks the vegetables. As Ron concedes, "This garden is a bit less focused on rigorous design than ones I design for clients, but it targets other goals that I enjoy on a personal level." He continues: "The farm garden is more experimental, less formal; it evolves more as time goes along and it is less static. Also I have built up the complexity with a specific intention of maximising the number of pollinator plants that we have for our local insects. It has been really successful in that regard, although that naturally results in a more relaxed, even bordering on chaotic, feeling in the planting. But I love it."

A more formal garden, with a conceptual theme, is the 'Sustainability Garden' Ron designed for a private research facility in California, where university scholars will study the local ecology. With this in mind, Ron created a four-hectare landscape that tells the story of the ecology (see pp. 98-9). It addresses the type of vegetation, the topography, hydrology and soil type – the inherent ecological principals of the region – and incorporates them into a garden. He does this with native plants paired with modern design. It is a distillation in miniature of the surrounding area with its mountains, foothills and the Sacramento River.

The area is next to a wetland, so Ron created a low spot within the site, took the spoil and made a fescue-covered, conical mound, and directed all the water down the mound in a cascade into a low, long, sweeping channel. This central watercourse meanders through a series of stone terraces of golden colour, reflecting the light and heat of the area, before being released into the existing wetland. In the same way that water drains off the mountain ranges in winter, helping to irrigate California, the basin-shaped garden experiences considerable flooding, but the stepped terraces planted with deer grasses can withstand this. The garden displays Lutsko's central interests: it combines an informative narrative, ecological integrity, and practicality. And it does this with drama and beauty.

Another wonderful project of Ron's is the garden for a private residence in Ketchum, Idaho. Ron says of this, "I love that garden, but I am a bit surprised it has got so much attention, because the idea behind it is so simple." He was on site with one of his associates, Laura, and to their eyes, as they looked at all the neighbouring gardens with small lawns and little spruce

trees and beds of flowers, they felt that the most interesting plots were the ones as yet undeveloped and undersigned, with no cultivated garden. Then Ron met the client, and he asked her why she had chosen to move to Ketchum. Her response was to take Ron and Laura on a hike into the native landscape, which is gorgeous. Her house, built largely of concrete and glass, backs onto a beautiful hill and Ron decided to use all the native plants growing there, sweeping the same planting throughout the garden.

The result is a site-sensitive, water-friendly garden where the bold, sharp features of the house and hard landscaping are complemented by the naturalistic, billowing planting. As the garden comes close to the house, Ron distills the wild plants from about fifteen species down to one or two. In these courtyard-like areas, Ron's Japanese influence is clearly evident. Here Ron asked Ned Kahn, an environmental artist and sculptor, to make a gate from white aluminum squares attached to a steel rod. The space is simple and serene: the gate is translucent; but when the wind blows, the squares flutter (see p.106).

Equally striking, and also fitting naturally into its surroundings, is a roof terrace designed for a private house in San Francisco. Here the basic form, scale and geometry was derived very strongly from Ron's desire to pull the pattern of the distant view of the city into the garden. However, in contrast to almost all of Ron's other work, this garden is filled with water-loving plants and it is introspective and meditational. This is because it is a small garden in the middle of the city, where privacy was required and the concept is more akin to a Japanese courtyard garden.

All Ron's designs explore and express the relationships between people's lives and their environments. So when it comes to having his own garden, Ron says, "It enables me to get in touch with the processes of design, to experiment, to feel nature a little more, and not be as worried about the constraints of other people's desires and agendas."

Just the colours white, silver and green create this fabulous roof terrace. Straight lines and one dramatic curve achieve perfect balance.

SHUNMYO **MASUNO**

There is a Zen proverb saying that when a venomous snake drinks water, it changes into poison; when a cow drinks water, it changes into milk. Shunmyo Masuno believes that it is up to him whether the same water he drinks is changed into poison or milk. As he says, "If my heart is not at rest, I cannot create beautiful gardens filled with spirituality. Therefore such gardens are also a mirror of myself. They are myself."

This concept is central to Masuno's work as an internationally acclaimed garden designer. He is head of Japan Landscape Consultants (JLC) and is also head priest at the sixteenth-century Kenkoh-ji Temple in Yokohama. This combination might at first seem strange (in fact the business side is run by Masuno's lay brother), but Zen priests have traditionally communicated their spiritual experiences through a classical art form, such as calligraphy or ikebana (flower arrangement). Zen priests who practise the art of landscape gardening are known as *ishidate-so*. However, Masuno is the last of his order still engaged in garden creation.

It is Masuno's belief that the spirit of seeking truth holds more importance than the act of garden making, and yet the two, for him, are intertwined. Through the practice of Zen, a state of mind is found that cannot be easily conveyed in words. One means of expressing it is in creating a garden, a place that mirrors the mind of the designer. Masuno, blue-robed, smiling and softly spoken, has an aura of timelessness, confidence and calm, so it is perhaps not surprising that his gardens induce a similar atmosphere.

Masuno was born in Kenkoh-ji Temple in 1953, the first child of a seventeenth-generation priest, Daikan Shinpo. Shunmyo grew up in the temple, knowing from a young age that he would become a priest; he was ordained in 1966. He graduated from the Department of Agriculture at Tamagawa University in 1975, and became an apprentice of landscape designer Katsuo Saito. He founded JLC Ltd in 1982, became head priest in 2001, and received an honorary degree from the University of British Columbia in 2005. Masuno still lives in Kenkoh-ji Temple, which also houses the design practice that he founded. When he was a child, Kenkoh-ji Temple had no garden. When he was about ten years old, his uncle got married in Kanazawa, and Masuno's parents took him to the ceremony, visiting Kyoto on the way back. Masuno saw the great temple gardens and was bowled over by them, dreaming that one day he might have a garden.

When Masuno was sixteen, Katsuo Saito, referred to by Masuno as 'my master', made the garden at Kenkoh-ji Temple. Masuno helped to build it, under Saito's guidance. He recalls, "It was a very important time for me. Saito was nearly 90 at that

time, but when we had coffee breaks he never let me relax. He always told me, 'Think of 20 different kinds of arrangements with those stones.' Then, after the coffee break he would ask me to tell him my arrangements. Then I would place the stones, but under his direction. He taught me that supervision at the construction site is very important." Thus the Kenkoh-ji Temple garden is not, strictly speaking, designed by Masuno. Nevertheless he thinks of it as 'his' garden and since its completion in 1976, he has chosen to change it hardly at all, "although the trees have grown and developed, because they have their own minds".

In Japan, it is thought that each tree and stone has its own soul, or inner life, which can be reawakened. As Masuno explains, "We have to think how each stone and tree would prefer to be set out. So a lot of experience and Japanese sensibility are required to create a true Japanese garden." Without Zen practice, Masuno warns, a Zen garden cannot be created; it will simply be an imitation. As well as placement, the choice of the perfect stone and rock is crucial. The result may appear minimal, since the ornamental is largely omitted, but it is actually philosophical, because the elemental remains. Masuno considers both creating and viewing gardens to be his most critical moments of ascetic practice.

Every morning, at around 5.00 a.m. Masuno opens the sliding doors to his temple garden. Though he does not have as much time to maintain the garden himself as he would wish, he likes to see the seasonal changes day by day. He says, "I often view the temple garden and check the situation of my mind." Because he is so accustomed to this garden, having seen it for most of his life, he has learned from it and been encouraged by it. And because it was not designed for a client, it is a garden that is to his own personal taste.

Kenkoh-ji Temple is in a residential, low-rise area of Yokohama. One enters the grounds first through woodland, where straight, green columns of bamboo imposingly surround the ceremonial bell house. The garden behind is reached through the temple building. Sliding doors (often left open) reveal what might be considered a quintessential Japanese garden. It is surrounded by small hills, which

PREVIOUS SPREAD: Viewed from the temple, the garden has balanced symmetry. *Phyllostachys* 'Mousou-Chiku' (bamboo) on the left is echoed by the *Acer palmatum* (Japanese maple) on the right. A semi-circle of round stones is repeated in the curved bridge.

OPPOSITE: Shunmyo Masuno stands in the garden of his temple, the cornerstone of his life, where he was born and is now head priest.

are utilised in the design, making the garden appear larger with this 'borrowed' backdrop. Within, is a semi-circle of round stepping stones, small pebbles, large rocks, a lantern, a statue, a waterfall and stream, maples, bamboo, moss and an arching bridge. The impression (in winter) is of green and grey; the sensation is of balance and harmony as well as an underlying tension.

The garden is both calm and strong, in that at first it seems very natural, and yet on inspection everything is controlled, ordered and meticulously placed. As Masuno explains, "The arrangement of the stones and the other elements in the garden combine with the existing trees to make a quiet

atmosphere. At the same time, the strong stone arrangement makes us tense." In this way the garden mirrors the Zen principle that initial calmness can lead to stimulated senses and a reinvigorated spirit. Masuno says, "My designs express my mind; they are not ends in themselves. I am bold enough to say that my mind is a place of contemplation. My temple garden makes me forget urban bustle. It is the best place for me to be relaxed and refreshed."

It transports the visitor too. People are able to view the garden before attending a Buddhist ceremony in the temple, so Masuno hopes that they, also, will gain calmness. There is a

Natural lush woodland contrasts with the perpendicular culms of bamboo. A sense of expectation is awakened, as one is led onwards to the front of Kenkoh-ji Temple.

LEFT: In front of the temple are a small wooden shrine and a ceremonial bell, housed in a pagoda.

NEXT SPREAD: Climbing the hill, looking back at the screened doors of the temple. Beneath are *Acer palmatum*, *A. palmatum* 'Bloodgood', cherry, camellia, small stones and large rocks, all placed perfectly.

strong tradition in Japanese garden design of the exterior and interior making one unified space (a fusion of man and nature). Indeed, Masuno sees gardens not as adjuncts to buildings, but as one component of the whole. In addition to being seen from inside, Kenkoh-ji Temple is a strolling garden, which can be entered (unlike some Zen gardens). A defined route is taken along paths and stepping-stones (which prevent guests soiling their footwear or their kimonos). The bridge acts as focal point, but also provides another vantage point from which to view the garden. Bamboos are simple, yet add sound and movement as their slender leaves rustle in the breeze.

As is often the case in Zen gardens, there is no seating within it, but the garden is often contemplated indoors, from the *tatami* (traditional mat) room, or from the viewing platform along the outside of the temple. This enables one to see the garden as a whole, almost as a picture or work of art. Western gardens are often places for activities such as growing produce and new plants, playing games or alfresco dining. Zen gardens are reflective places that remain visually much the same from one year to another. Here the mind can focus. If you know what the various elements in the garden represent, so much the better, but it is not a necessary part of appreciating the whole. In the Kenkoh-ji Temple garden, the three large rocks are called *Sanzonseki* and the arrangement

expresses Buddha and his two apprentices. The statue is Ojizousama, the guardian angel to all human beings, but especially to children (hence the red cap symbolising the caul or placenta).

There are also many trees and shrubs in this garden. Masuno tells me, "Temples and shrines are the best places to create and preserve traditional gardens, although if a building is in the old style it is still suited to a traditional garden. Kenkoh-ji had lots of greenery already present in its setting. To utilise the characteristics of the site is one of the most important factors of design in Japan. But conditions change. Now many buildings are made with concrete and are very tall. While gardens used to be seen from a *tatami* mat, they might now be viewed from a chair, for example in a hotel lobby, and if the eye-level changes, the designer must take this into account."

There are three main kinds of Zen gardens. *Karensansui* is a dry-stone garden where an arrangement of stones, gravel and moss is viewed from a specified point, often for meditation. *Tsukiyama* is a strolling garden (such as Kenkoh-ji Temple) where the visitor wanders along paths encouraging contemplation of nature outside the garden. *Chaniwa* is a tea garden where the emphasis is on the

Three pyramids traverse part of the north edge of the Canadian Embassy, representing the Rocky Mountains.

OPPOSITE: The Embassy benefits from borrowed views of a wooded park. Spanning the long eastern terrace is the Canada Garden. Beneath the projecting roof (which compresses the visual frame to a panorama) the large stones, left in the rough state in which they split, convey the ancient Canadian Shield, gouged by glaciers.

teahouse and traditional tea ceremony. All these types of garden rely on simplicity, and part of the process of design is to remove extraneous elements. When Masuno designs for clients, he uses all three styles. He has received accolades for his more orthodox renovation of the 'Nitobe Memorial Garden' in Vancouver and his 'Yuusien Garden' in Berlin, but he also designs more experimental *Karensansui*. These appear very different from his temple garden: they have little or no greenery and considerably more drama.

As a Zen priest, Masuno has not withdrawn from the modern world, but has embraced it in his contemporary approach to his designs for the modern metropolis. Masuno maintains that when people live in urban centres, crowded and under the

pressure of work, a garden can offer relief from daily stress and even a means for recovery of one's basic humanity. In cities there is often limited space for a garden, especially one that has enough space to walk round. Most of the gardens in the Muromachi era (AD 1333-1568) are viewed from inside; but it is not only ancient temples, but also skyscrapers and modern architecture, that are particularly well suited to *Karensansui* style. Masuno confirms this when he says, "Buildings made of concrete, metal and glass are sharp architecturally, so the garden should also be composed sharply. In that case, I often use hewn stone."

For the Cerulean Tower Hotel, Masuno created a 'Garden of Waves' where the movement and flow of water is strikingly represented by dry rocks and stones. It is viewed from the sunken, circular lobby lounge, which Masuno also conceived. The design for the garden of the Canadian Embassy in Aoyama, Tokyo (see pp.118-9), was entrusted to Masuno in 1901. He immediately saw that the garden had to relate to the people who worked in the embassy and to visitors. He said he wanted "to encourage people to reappraise their roles". So the garden, in two linked areas, symbolises the relationship between Canada (the larger area) and Japan (the smaller). *Karesansui* was ideal for this conceptual approach, and Masuno exploited his love of stone to emphasise the geology of Canada, using granite stones brought from Hiroshima prefecture. They had to be labouriously hollowed out to overcome the structural problem of their weight. The garden representing Japan is a Zen garden of natural stones, raked gravel and stepping-stones in a geometric design, indicating formality and control.

This shallow pond, viewed from the coffee shop in Hotel Le Port, represents the floor of a Japanese tea ceremony room. Within it are eleven dynamically cut stones (odd numbers are felicitous). The backdrop, equivalent to a scroll painting, is a waterfall terrace made of two kinds of stone.

OPPOSITE: Here the different stones are seen in close up: brown granite rocks support thinly sliced South African black granite slabs, chiselled at the edges. The combination creates diverse breaks in the cascades of sparkling water.

A waterfall is often an important part of a Zen garden (a barrier to overcome before a higher stage of consciousness) and it is the primary element in the garden of the Kojimachi Kaikan (Le Port) Hotel. As with the National Research Institute at Tsukuba, Masuno often uses contemporary and sophisticated water features. At Hotel Le Port, Masuno comments, "Landscape for this project was very limited, but scale is not an important factor for me. Each garden's concept is derived from Zen thought." The area is seen through windows in the coffee shop, so Masuno created a Modernist interpretation of a *tokanama*, an alcove in a tea-ceremony room where objects of aesthetic significance, such as a scroll painting, are placed. At the hotel, in a narrow channel, a waterfall cascades down precisely carved, granite slabs. Stones are cut unnaturally and a tension is created that seems to relate conceptually to the human psyche rather than the natural world. In gardens such as these, Masuno manages to preserve the ancient art of Zen garden design, while at the same time proving the form's viability, relevance and huge influence on global landscape design in the twenty-first century.

Much has been written about the philosophy behind Japanese gardens, such as the idea that nature is sacred; the importance of parables and metaphors for self-enlightenment; deceptive perspective; viewpoint and composition; and the merging of inside and out. Although many of these elements are emulated in Western design, they can seem daunting. If, however, you follow Masuno's beliefs, things become much simpler. He stresses that it is not form but the atmosphere that fills the space, which is important. If this is the case, then perhaps the garden of Kenkoh-ji Temple is not as dissimilar from most of Masuno's commissioned work as it might appear.

The atmosphere in a well-designed Zen garden is palpable. It may contain the frisson of contrasts, but it is ultimately calming and uplifting. Masuno strives to express his spiritual self through garden design. In achieving this, all his gardens convey that spirituality to the visitor as well. They are places in which the mind dwells, where people become moved by the expression of the designer. Or as Muso Soseki, another famous Zen priest who expressed himself through landscape, wrote in the thirteenth century, "There is nothing special in water and mountain, there is special only in the minds of people."

DAN **PEARSON**

It is fitting that I first met Dan Pearson at an RHS flower show in London (he was buying nerines and *Lilium martagon*), since he is a horticulturalist, and his garden in Peckham, South London, is clearly that of a plantsman. He is also an internationally respected landscape designer, broadcaster, lecturer and writer. Dan's interest in gardening started as a child, when his father dug a pond in their garden. It developed further when he became friendly with a retired teacher, Geraldine, who lived nearby and was a keen naturalist and gardener. Later Dan trained at RHS Wisley and at the Royal Botanic Gardens, Kew, before starting his professional career as a designer in 1987. Now Dan Pearson Studio handles both private gardens and public spaces in Britain and abroad.

Having studied wildflowers in Spain and the Himalayas, and having spent two years working in the Botanic Gardens of Jerusalem and Edinburgh respectively, Dan has a great under-standing of how plants relate to their surroundings. This, combined with a deep appreciation of nature, an inspired ability to organise space, and a unique sensitivity to the spirit of a place, are the qualities that inform his work.

Dan has a calm, slightly ethereal quality about him and so does his garden. It lies behind a row of unremarkable terraced Victorian houses, and is 38 metres × 11 metres, southwest facing, with alluvial soil. It is divided into five areas on three levels – these can be used more easily than a long thin rectangle, and also provide a series of experiences that can be dipped into. The two bottom terraces are like antechambers between the house and garden. Sliding glass doors from the wooden-floored basement open onto a mobau wood deck.

The first plant to greet you on entering the garden is a *Cercis canadensis* 'Forest Pansy', planted in a huge terracotta bowl. Dan bought the plant twelve years ago, choosing this specimen for its already slanting trunk. It is now growing at a 45-degree angle, and he has pruned it to frame the garden, like a tilted umbrella of large, deep-purple, heart-shaped leaves. It is dramatic, simple and stunning, leaving a lasting impression. From inside, in the kitchen, the tree creates a sense of reveal, in that you do not see the garden all at once. The glass doors also

frame the tree, so that as Dan says, "It forms its own picture". The tree, moreover, has all the seasons in it. In winter, you can see through it, in spring buds burgeon, and in the summer months the garden disappears again, before the leaves turn a glorious bronze, followed by yellow, and then fall to the ground in the autumn.

This tree sets the stage for the whole garden, where the sum is more than its parts and harmony pervades throughout. Beneath the 'Forest Pansy' is a terracotta pan of clear, reflecting water. Dan comments memorably, "I like bringing the sky down to earth". He has used still water, as well as Perspex spheres, to mirror clouds in his commissioned gardens and Chelsea shows, but on a larger scale. He loves the water bowls in his own garden and watches them, knowing whether it is raining without having to go outside. Up a cantilevered step from this lowest terrace is one paved in limestone. On the right is an inviting, secluded wooden table and bench, backed by a huge screen of rustling, swaying, black bamboo. When Dan talks about gardens sharpening the senses, one can see why.

Beyond is a path of silvery, slatey, limestone chippings. There is no lawn, but relaxed, dense planting. Lime-green *Nasturtium* 'Mahogany' leaves spill over the path, while further along, autumn grasses and seedheads sway amongst the mid-green, elliptical leaves of *Persicaria virginiana*, each marked with a maroon 'V'. The showy flowers of *Nicotiana sylvestris* and *N. mutabilis* cavort with stunning, one-and-a-half metre, *Impatiens tinctoria* with its white, long-spurred flowers, magenta-stained at the mouth. These were a present from Great Dixter and, as soon as I admired them, Dan gave me a cutting.

Further along is a second decked terrace, or 'clearing' as Dan calls it, on which stands a copper, filled with water, this time with a lily in it. It is placed beside wooden chairs, shaded by a hornbeam taken from one of Dan's Chelsea gardens. In fact the design of his own garden originally revolved around a large, silvery-leaved pineapple broom (*Cytisus battandieri*), but fungus killed it, so in 2004, the hornbeam, which Dan regards as a neutral tree, replaced it. There are plants in this garden from South America, India, the Himalayas, China, Japan and Europe, and he wanted a tree that would absorb all those differences and allow everything to shine around it. Choosing the hornbeam represented a significant change, consolidating the process of making a personal garden that was not entirely site-specific (reliant on enhancing a mood set by pre-existing features).

Dan does make use of the surrounding gardens, however. Boundaries are frayed and almost concealed, as the eye leads

you onwards to where in autumn, Virginia Creeper, hanging over the wall from the garden next door, glows and mimics the flowers of red dahlias planted by Dan beneath. Here too, pots are stored and a cold frame resides, bordered by raised beds holding herbs and salads. Dan also has a separate allotment nearby, and has turned the garage of his house into a potting shed. Finally, a path of stepping-stones leads through a shady area at the back of the garden to the compost heap. These stones are actually formed from the original concrete path that ran through the garden: a deliberate link with the past.

What Dan has attempted and achieved is a balance in his garden between a space that is tranquil and beautiful and that can indulge his love of unusual plants, with an experimental think tank that generates ideas for clients' gardens. Additionally, his garden is a social space for family and friends, who use it a lot. The large table is for eating outside: "We are very rarely inside in the summer. It is not just a garden space. It is where we live." Dan spends a lot of time gardening too, explaining: "I am very territorial about my weekends. People sometimes ask, 'Do you have any help in your garden?' and it always makes me laugh because it just wouldn't feel right. It is quite a lot of work and I need to spend at least half a day every week on it. I love that. I couldn't function without it. I trained as a gardener – it is totally different from doing a design and plant layout for contractors. This is where I can get my hands dirty."

This garden is very personal and Dan is much freer with colour here than he is when commissioned by other people. Nevertheless, he has achieved his goal of unity and balance with the occasional surprise. In general (though rules are sometimes broken here) he reserves blues, mauves and whites for the shady parts of the garden (as in woodland) where they can glow unbleached by sun. Bright, hot colours intensify in sun, and in Dan's garden in summer, hues sizzle and flare, pushing boundaries. Although his general advice is that people should always edit and reduce their plant lists and allow tranquil greens to predominate, the schemes in his own garden (drawing on the Arts and Crafts gardening ethos reinterpreted as new naturalism) are exciting and, sometimes, serendipitous results of self-seeding.

OPPOSITE: Strong verticals of green *Papaver somniferum* (a single black poppy Dan has had since childhood, bearing seedheads here) and grey/green *Eryngium giganteum* are striking against the softer masses of *Geranium* 'Patricia' and the clusters of maroon *Sanguisorba* 'Tanna'.

Clients, Dan says, generally do not understand this and would not tolerate the apparent disorder. But he likes the fact that here, anything can happen. He engages with nature, riding it, steering it gently, but it has the upper hand. His garden is not ordered and controlled but has a deliberately informal mood. In spring, admittedly, the garden is neater. Then Dan's love of special treasures, such as trilliums and brown irises (disliked by some clients) come to the fore. He thrives on the series of waves that break over the year. As he comments, although gardens are actually a massive contrivance, they also have their own order.

Dan has owned this garden since 1997, when it had been neglected for ten years. He bought the house in Peckham because you can get more outside space for your money there than in other parts of London, and as soon as he saw the garden, he thought, 'This is it!' He walked to the end of the plot, and only then looked back through the brambles to see a large, dilapidated house in which students had lived. Within a month, he had bought it. He simplified the house, but found designing his own garden one of the hardest things he had ever done (he had previously lived in a flat with a small roof terrace). There were so many plants he wanted to grow and myriad possibilities. So he spent time waiting, testing the soil, watching the seasons and the movement of light. He likes to be aware of what time of day it is in the garden, and of the elements, and for all his senses to be stimulated – to find ways of engaging with the natural world. Only after a year did Dan develop a plan. He excavated 35 tons of soil, clearing brambles and creating the terraces, before planting the garden.

To start with he was inundated with greenfly and blackfly because by removing all the brambles and growth that was there before, he had also erased the ecology. It took over a year for that to come back, and now he never sprays and everything is organic. He does use glyphosate, diligently, when necessary, and organic slug bait, carefully, where needed. One thing he cannot control is a problem with foxes – digging, crashing and smashing as well as coming into the house and stealing shoes!

Dan also refrained from planting any bulbs for over a year because once they are planted it is harder to make other changes. Now there are lots, especially fine-leaved narcissus,

nectaroscordums, irises, trilliums, arismæmas, anemones, and alliums. He also has lilies, planted near the front of the beds so he can pick off the lily beetles. Dan admits to finding plants hard to resist and says that when he compares his plant list from when he first took over this garden with his current one, it is almost completely different.

The wisteria at the back of the house (the first plant Dan introduced), the bamboo and the fig tree have remained from his original scheme. Some plants, however, were fatalities. He planted a screen of *Salix exigua* (Coyote willow) that for six years formed a veil through which the end of the garden was seen. It had a lovely, shimmery lightness but then suddenly, because the willows prefer sandy soil and the soil is so rich here, they started falling over and splitting. Once they split they started getting fungal infections and Dan was unable to re-establish them. He believes strongly that quite a lot of plants other than roses suffer from replant disease. After three years, he gave up and replanted with *Sambucus nigra* (elder) to great effect.

However, Dan says that if he were staying for another five years, he would not keep the elder, but would replace it with something else. It was planted, in part, as a trial for other people's plots, but is becoming quite a common plant in gardens, and interestingly, Dan would take it out now, because you are starting to see it everywhere. He would rather have something that you see less often in his own space. He will also remove plants if he tires of them after living with them every day. "I am hungry for plant experiences that are truly satisfying. Certain plants are able to provide something for you at every point in the year and other plants aren't. And the mood is so particular here that there are only certain things that fit, and finding them is not always easy."

Dan concedes that his garden has definitely been influenced by his time in Japan (he has created fabulous gardens in Tokyo and Hokkaido); it has a similar spirit, although his is not in any way a Japanese garden. It is, however, like a Japanese forest, because many of the plants might be found there; it is relaxed, like a woodland floor though it is not a woodland; it is like a meadow where it is open, but not like a British meadow because it is not as

dry and feels almost like the Pampas, or somewhere with high rainfall. The aesthetic is curiously lush, but it is definitely not exotic.

Although Dan occasionally uses exotic plants in his designs for others, he personally feels that if something performs for 365 days in the same way, it is boring. For example, while acknowledging that astelias are beautiful, and recalling that he once had them in his garden, where they grew enormous and loved the conditions, he tired of them. On the other hand, he does have box mounds. These, although constant, have a flush of new growth in spring, which is an amazing colour. "For a moment," he says, "even only two weeks, it is as though a light has been switched on." Some other plants that have stayed, such as *Rosa x oderata* 'Mutabilis', *Hydrangea aspera, Euphorbia mellifera*, Dan claims he would never take out, because he has had them long enough to know that he loves them.

I visited this private garden just as Dan was about to move to a 9-hectare smallholding in Somerset, in which, he says, he will play a smaller part. There will inevitably be a process of loss but

he is also excited about having a completely new challenge. He would like his new plot to be about a journey. There will be a garden hugging the house, but he hopes not to see that when you stroll further away. Pearson, like Perazzi, is increasingly interested in embracing wildness within the man-made environments of his art. He would like his new garden to be simpler. Using an analogy with music, Dan explains that he has learnt to use fewer notes.

Some plants, nevertheless, are potted in Peckham, ready to be taken to their new home. Examples are the Paeonia 'Late Windflower', which was a present from Beth Chatto, and some nerines given to Dan by his old friend, Geraldine, which have flowered in each of his own gardens. The 'Forest Pansy', however (although in a large pot), is staying because it is too essential a feature of the garden to remove.

Dan's garden is an oasis in the city: a sensual space that immerses him. Like other art forms, it provides a heightened awareness. It gives him a feeling of being transported to a place where anything can happen, as in meditation. It is cerebral as well as physical. Dan's is a London garden, but it is not about London at all, and is therefore a contrast to the rest of his work, which is largely site-generated. Here, tuning into the existing place, he has created a new one. He has even

incorporated the sound of rustling foliage to distract from that of sirens. Admittedly he has 'borrowed' greenery from adjoining gardens, but this adds a sense of space. He has created a non-urban environment.

For clients, whether it is a roof garden that celebrates the roofscape, or a forest garden, or somewhere with a view, or water, or a particular tree that is magical, or a landform or building, the mood and atmosphere of the garden is dictated by what is already there. In his own garden, Dan wanted to create an antidote to an environment and energy that he finds challenging and exhausting. His success bears testament to his skill as a garden designer. He also writes beautifully, and in his book *Spirit*, he ends an essay about Rousham (William Kent's inspirational garden): 'Your walk unfolds in your mind's eye whilst you ponder whether you want to make your way back into the real world.' The same might be said about Dan's garden.

Opposite: 'Tokachi Millennium Forest', Hokkaido, is a 200-hectrare site, designed to be sustainable for 1000 years. Including a visitor centre and restaurant, it shows Dan's work on a totally different scale. But the stunning, soft, naturalistic planting is typical of his work.

Above: In another part of the 'Millennium Forest' sculpted landforms, mirroring the hills of the surrounding northern Japanese landscape, take your breath away.

Post Script

Since writing the previous pages, Dan has moved. Feeling that he had outgrown his Peckham garden, his new, expansive plot consists of glorious, rolling pastureland surrounding a small, neglected house. I met Dan, secateurs in his hand, in the only bit of 'garden' cultivated by the previous owner – a vegetable patch. Here, beside his few Peckham plants, Dan is trialling different varieties of herbs and vegetables (his aim is to become completely self-sufficient). In his London garden, Dan had few native plants and more species than cultivars (such as irises from the Himalayas and roses from China) although they all had a wild, naturalistic look. In Somerset, Dan is collecting plants and seeds with local provenance. But he also pined for more blowsy flowers and planted 40 different bearded irises and 20 different David Austin roses within his formal enclosure, which does not impose on the landscape. He explains that he is expanding his horticultural experience and experimenting on behalf of clients.

Dan has now planned out how the garden will work. "I will move the old vegetable patch to the other side of the house, so that on arrival, you will not see it. At first there will be no challenge of garden for your mind, and it will be a surprise." So far, he has planted a great many young trees in the landscape (an orchard, nuttery and blossom walk, as well as ash trees that spear the hedges) but he is pacing himself with the rest of the

planting and landscaping of this new space. Some herbaceous plants will be grown within rounded enclosures of park railing in the meadow, each with a slightly different shape and character, such as sun-filled with air and light, or shade and moisture-loving plants by the brook and willows. Dan explains that this idea is not dissimilar from the roundels used by 'Capability' Brown (1716–1783) who used them with trees to create shade for animals or put them on the tops of hills to make them higher, merging them with the landscape.

Much of the land will flow between these enclosures and be left for grazing, haymaking and wild flowers. Dan claims, "It is joyous to be working with the landscape rather than fiddling with gardening, although I will never not garden, because it is a means of measuring your relationship with nature. But I am finding a way of engaging with nature without gardening. It is wonderful and a hugely exciting process of discovery. For example, some of the grassland is really rich, not good for wild flowers. I have learned that in certain places, such as by hedges, where the livestock collected at nighttime, the animals would manure the ground over the years more heavily than anywhere else so that you can see patterns develop. I will play with that to either heighten or suppress what is happening in that space." This is a totally site-generated space and Dan is very interested in authenticity and, for example, restoring hedges to where they once were.

In Somerset, Dan is celebrating the unadorned. Everything, however, is carefully considered. The nuttery is planted on an offset grid so that it reappears and disappears as you move through it. As he says, "Sometimes you can see the grid and sometimes it just looks like an informal group of trees and I really enjoy that. And there are four different groups, working against each other like a textile." At the bottom of the valley is a stream and Dan is planning several different ways of crossing it: stepping-stones, fords and a variety of bridges enabling different experiences. This area was infested with brambles and nettles that Dan is clearing. He hopes to regenerate wild flowers and plant native daffodils here. He finds maintenance regimes that change the landscape fascinating, and something he would never be able to monitor in a client's garden.

Dan explains: "I am going through the same processes as I would for a client, but I think I am learning the language more intricately here, because you can only assume so much about a site you have only visited a few times. When you are living a site, looking every day, it is different." Dan concludes, "Gardens are not actually relaxing, because one is always wanting to change things, or mourning something that has died, but this landscape is soul food, and it is where I want to be."

Both of Dan's plots, despite being experimental, share a spiritual atmosphere enabling communication with nature. In Peckham this was on a small scale; in Somerset it is on a very large one. Both spaces are extremely personal. When Geraldine, Dan's childhood mentor, died, she left him a small amount of money. As she loved blossom and berries, he has used her legacy to buy 500 whips of trees such as hawthorn and sorbus that will develop into a blossom wood along the ridge of the land. So although this is the start of a new era for Dan, it is also as though his journey is coming full-circle.

OPPOSITE: A grid of hazel trees, protected from sheep, enhances this field; it forms part of the stunning scenery that is Dan's current landscape.

LEFT: Dan loves the natural patterns that appear in this lush area of hillside.

BELOW LEFT: Because the intensive grazing on this tump has been slackened, it is already beginning to show huge potential in terms of wild flowers. On the horizon are ash trees. There is a tradition of pollarding ash in this area, which Dan will continue.

BELOW RIGHT: Pearson explains that as his work is increasingly to do with landscape rather than garden, his move to the country was appropriate. He is keen to maintain a sense of a working farming valley and let the meadow come right up to the house.

ANTONIO **PERAZZI**

It is Antonio Perazzi's philosophy and approach to garden design that make his gardens special. His innovative environmental stance and in-depth knowledge of botany inform all his work, whether in Italy, Switzerland, the US or Kuwait. His focus is unequivocally on plants rather than hard landscaping; he is particularly interested in the energy of plants, especially wild ones that are ever-evolving in their quest to adapt to an environment artificially created by man. Perazzi has been practising landscape design since 1992, opening his own studio in Milan in 1996. He creates public and private gardens as well as temporary installations for leading international exhibitions and has won many awards. He also lectures widely on environmental architecture.

Antonio's own garden is in Piuca, a somewhat remote hamlet near Greve in Chianti. Set against a glorious backdrop of hills and vineyards, it exemplifies his belief that contemporary gardens should be more and more like nature itself, an evolving biological organism, with only slight, respectful design. In 1988 Antonio was left 2.5 hectares of land and a farmhouse by his grandfather, a strong socialist and fighter against fascism, who lived in an adjacent house. Antonio's aunt was a famous radical journalist (and perhaps

some of his own revolutionary views are inherited). His mother still lives in the house adjoining Antonio's garden, which originally was uncultivated, overgrown land. Antonio loved this wild place as a child: the house where he and his family now spend weekends and holidays was inhabited by domestic and wild animals.

When Antonio inherited the property, he was a poor student and had to renovate the house and land slowly, with little help. Now the stone building has become a typical, simple but attractive Tuscan family home, and the land, which slopes down from the house, is a

PREVIOUS SPREAD: Produce from the garden is important to Antonio and his family. Shown here, some just-picked raspberries and rhubarb, placed on the terrace wall, create a still life with the valerian that romps over the roof.

BELOW: Looking back towards the house, the glow of the setting sun warms the patch of long grass and wild flowers left unmown in this softly textured quilt of meadow.

OPPOSITE: Steps lead from the house to the garden, with lavender and hydrangea to the side. Benedetta is carrying their five-week-old daughter. The dog, rescued from a motorway, is never far from Antonio.

communities that thrive together without constant control by gardeners or chemicals. When Antonio cleared the ground in Piuca, he detected deep wet areas and stony, calcareous sites. He found terraces hidden beneath the undergrowth near the house. He had no overall plan for the garden, which developed in stages, but the natural configuration of the land was always respected, and soil was not added or removed.

No seed mix was added to the meadows, but different wild flowers appear each year in the changing areas that are left un-mown. Homogeneous patches of daisies, vetches, cornflowers, thyme, wild orchids, and even viburnums and strawberry trees, spring up miraculously. Until six years ago there were no fences, and still the garden provides shelter to many visiting wild animals. It is an open space facing the landscape: a place that receives the sunrise and the sunset. Nature, in every form, is welcomed into this garden that is not filled with razzmatazz, but is a charming, atmospheric, family space. Though on acquaintance, rather like an abstract painting, it delivers far more than the sum of its parts.

The garden is designed to be low maintenance, for Antonio is not always here. As he says, "I am grateful that even if I am away the garden is still here and healthy, waiting, like a dog for my return." But it is also rich in cultivated plants, many collected on Antonio's extensive travels, or given by fellow enthusiasts and botanists. There is a large collection of Mediterranean oaks, some grown from acorns (planted in autumn because in spring they die as there is no irrigation), and bamboos from a friend who has a nursery in France. There are also about 300 different species roses, more than 60 clematis, as well as peonies (some brought back from China), camellias, dahlias, crocosmia, dierama, hydrangeas, scabious (from Crete) vinca (found by Antonio in Japan) and many other flowering plants (including a lavatera from Great Dixter).

Antonio has learnt in which part of the garden each of these plants will thrive, or a certain situation will suggest a planting to him. For example, his Mediterranean cistus requires good drainage so he has planted it in a stony area. Exotic plants work in harmony with wild flowers and never overpower the spontaneous beauty of the place. In this sense, although his larger projects for clients are more formal, Perazzi is working against the aesthetic of traditional Italian gardens. He has largely rejected the classical ideals of order,

ABOVE: Wildlife and birds are encouraged here, in houses provided above the cosmos.

OPPOSITE: While this garden appears very natural, care is clear. The striking plumes of macleaya match the stone; the grey/green leaves are the exact tone of the painted shutters.

wonderful garden. Though it creates a relaxed, natural overall effect, it contains copious carefully positioned pots, a pergola, pond, plants, stream and woodland as well as a meadow with areas of wild flowers. Crossing a lane there is also a kitchen garden, successfully co-habited by flowers, vegetables and fragrant herbs.

The garden unfolds in a series of pictures framed by the surrounding vineyards, olive groves and forest, for in all Antonio now owns around 20 hectares. Different areas, and even neighbouring gardens merge and flow with connecting pathways. There are no straight lines, axes or obvious structure. There are also no flowerbeds (Antonio has discovered that the wind here causes evaporation, leaving soil depleted of goodness so there is no bare earth) and no lawn. The trees and shrubs as well as flowers, grow in meadow grass, which is left uncut in various organically shaped patches. Everything is artfully arranged, but this is a garden that is also partly redesigned by nature each year.

Plants are re-evaluated and used in a new way here, as in Antonio's commissioned gardens. Following on from the work of innovators such as the late Dutch gardener, writer and designer, Henk Gerritsen (1948–2008), Perazzi creates plant

where symmetry combined with extravagant fountains, statues and grottos impressed the world for centuries. In Italy, Antonio tells me, 'design' means something different from in England. With the market in designer furniture, especially in Milan, there is a new concept in Italy, where a designed garden refers to one with a lot of clearly visible modern elements and hard landscaping.

Antonio declares that there are several landscape architects working in Italy who ignore plants and the sense of the landscape completely. They are more on a par with interior designers. He, on the other hand, considers the site and the client, but says, "I could never make a tailor-made garden for a client because of my sense of respect for the landscape. There are other designers who have a very clear style that they can reproduce all over the world, but I find that difficult. I was once asked to design a garden for a lady who said that she was terrified of bees. So I said to her, 'I cannot make a garden without bees.' "

While Antonio enjoys living and working in Milan, he feels at home in Piuca, where he spends a lot of time gardening. He says his garden is very important to him, because it enables him

to study the cultivation of plants and their biological potential. For the last few years he has travelled a lot in China and Japan and believes that in relatively recent times, as buildings and roads developed through Asia, seeds from exotic wild plants were carried into Europe, and it is these which now shape our cultivated gardens. Seeing wild plants growing in Hunan, China, thrilled both him and his wife, Benadetta.

Antonio explains: "There is a new interest in the wilderness. Based on the history of the last 50 years, it is becoming evident that not all exotic plants are dangerous to our landscape. So we might be able to discover categories of powerful exotic plants that are not thugs that reduce biodiversity by reproducing more quickly than natives. For example, in Italy, we have an invasion of buddlejas (from China) growing up to

ABOVE: Self-seeded annuals: cosmos, hollyhocks, evening primrose and cow parsley feather the foreground.

OPPOSITE: Through the flowers of ceonothus, is a view of the sloping garden and hills beyond. The green glass balls, looking like sculpted apples, were saved from a local wine-maker.

3,000 metres, which is a problem because they hamper the drainage on the mountains. We also have ailanthus trees, which like very poor soil. However, I believe that actually some plants, over a number of years, just move around the landscape, finding places where they can grow and sometimes improve the soil and increase biodiversity."

Antonio enjoys the ability to work physically and think philosophically in his garden. He also uses it as a laboratory in which to study plants before using them in clients' gardens. Often worried and frustrated by what might happen after his design is complete and he has left, he aims to create gardens that, like his own, are sustainable. However, it is common in Italy for a landscape architect to do the design but then not be involved in the build, so that he cannot be sure that his choices will be realised.

Recently, Antonio won a competition to design a public project in Milan, but by the time it was built everything had changed. He had calculated levels to make maintenance easier, but in the end it was flattened. On the other hand, he is about to start work on another project he won, to landscape a large portion of fast-track railway line, where he will be giving instruction to the engineers who will do the construction. He is pleased and

optimistic about this, saying, "It will involve a perception of the landscape, seeing it from the outside and from the inside as a passenger on the train. And I will also incorporate some exotic plants that have arrived into Italy."

Antonio describes designing a garden as similar to being a chef, saying, "You play with sensation, with emotions and with a sentimental approach to something very physical. It is like preparing an elaborate dish. Ideally you should understand all the flavours and the history of the ingredients. The person eating the food need not necessarily understand this to enjoy the food; you can surprise, so long as it still tastes good."

He goes on to say, "One of the things I like most about my profession is the chance to understand a lot of different ecologies, societies and plants. Gardens and landscapes are contradictory terms and should exhibit different characteristics; one is designed and constructed, and the other is wild and unpredictable. But they share one thing in common and that is plants. I believe gardens are an expression of culture and of being a part of society at a particular time. Creating a garden is not just an exercise in style or ostentation, but gives the possibility of having a relationship with something much bigger than ourselves."

Antonio studies plants and is also a plant-hunter. For instance, around the small studio that occupies a position at the top end of the garden, are many Sicilian grasses, euphorbias and broom, brought back when he did a project around Mount Etna, on volcanic soil. They thrive in his garden, having no irrigation and being left to their own devices. Antonio's ideal is to enable people who are not extremely rich to fulfill their dreams of owning a beautiful garden without a gardener, as they (unlike garden designers) are very highly paid in Italy. Another of his cost-saving devices is to plant very small trees, which are inexpensive, but can delight the owner as they grow.

He also encourages the growing of produce. Antonio is proud to make his own olive oil, as well as jam from his raspberries, and I can assert that his Sicilian mulberry tree bore the most luscious fruit I have ever tasted. When Bruno, his eldest son, was small and watched his father dig up potatoes, he would go all round the garden digging, expecting to find potatoes, like buried treasure. The pleasure of the father is clear, though he admits that if he had the choice, he would not have selected this site for a garden because of its extremes in temperature in summer and winter, making cultivation difficult. But it has strong sentimental attachment with important family connections: he is close to his mother (who keeps chickens in her part of the garden) and it is a place where children from his present and previous marriage all enjoy themselves.

Antonio is devoted to his family. Though he has had some difficult times in his life, he is now content. He is also glad that he works side by side with Benedetta, who is a partner in his studio, and of whom he says, "She does not mind that I am deeply involved with my work but encourages me to follow my dream." Benadetta is supportive and hardworking, as well as beautiful. Bruno, his son by his first wife, climbs trees in the garden and Antonio built a house in one for him. Olmo (an ancient Tuscan name meaning elm tree), an affectionate toddler, plays in the grass in Piuca, while in the studio in Milan he investigates touching (and sometimes damaging) models. Antonio's eldest daughter comes to Piuca to relax; his new baby girl gets carried around the garden in a sling. As Antonio points out, "The garden of a landscape architect is a manifestation of his way of life. It is a hobby and a profession together. In my case it is a laboratory but it is also a place where I can grow plants that I like and which express my work. And it is a place that gives my family a chance to understand me." This last comment also perhaps applies to those lucky enough to visit.

Having spent most of the day with Antonio and his family, the following day he drove me to a garden he designed for a private client. It is still being built, just outside Bologna. At first sight this is very different from Piuca. The plot is large (and originally had no

Texture and colour, as well as straight and soft lines combine to wonderful effect in this client's garden. A hornbeam hedge surrounds a row of *Prunus* 'Royal Burgundy' enclosing airy *Verbena bonariensis* and translucent grasses.

OPPOSITE: This arresting, geometric kitchen garden outside Bologna is enhanced by views of the hills framed by the pergola.

garden); there are designated routes; the client (for whom Antonio has already made four previous gardens) is wealthy; and the garden, when finished, will be grand and impressive. Antonio, who by now is a friend of the owner and has even been on holiday with him, advised him on rebuilding the house, designating its orientation, and putting in windows that follow axes, creating a strong relationship with the garden from the inside.

This garden, designed on a series of terraces which have had to be made, is, in this respect, more what Antonio jokingly calls 'Capability Brown style'. On arrival, most of the house is concealed and the garden reveals itself in a series of surprises. As Antonio puts it, "I did not want the house, which is on a hill, to look like a candle on a cake, but to be integrated with the landscape." Close to the house, the garden is geometric, and has distinct 'rooms' but ever-present as part of the picture, are the voluptuous Mediterranean hills on one side of the site, and the flatter valley in which Bologna lies, on the other.

There is a large, beautiful kitchen garden, as well as flower gardens of colour-themed beds and collections of botanical roses, peonies, frost-resistant jasmines, and a collection of Mediterranean oaks (as there is in Piuca, but this one contains 70 species). Also included are a 'room' of edible berries, a 'room' for playing cards, and a large swimming pool: all for the pleasure of the owner, his clients and friends. Gardeners will tend this garden, whereas Antonio says, "My own garden is private and I feel it is my privilege to look after it." This garden also differs from all others designed by Antonio in that large trees were brought in by crane and planted. Some trees, however, such as the olives that line the drive, were saved and transplanted from a building site in Puglia. Antonio is against the practice of taking ancient olive trees out of the Southern Italian landscape to be sold by nurseries, as they then often slowly die in a new garden.

So this garden, too, adheres to Antonio's principals and philosophy. Only a few parts are irrigated and there is only a very small carpet of lawn by the house. Chemicals are used on the roses and oaks, but nowhere else. In one area, the plants are all indigenous, creating a corridor for insects, birds and animals from the garden to the surroundings. Texture and sensuous planting, as in Antonio's own garden, play an important part here. Moreover, as the levels change, so shapes become more flowing and rounded, with natural hedges, grasses rather than lawn and, of course, wild flowers. This is the part that Antonio says "gives back to the landscape and shows the importance of the relationship between wilderness and cultivated plants".

It follows that since Antonio is interested in ideas, some of his temporary garden installations are conceptual. For example, in his stunning 'Bluebois' for the International Garden Festival in Métis, Quebec, he investigated the creative process in landscape design. The garden was only there for a short time, but it expressed something of the omnipotence of building a garden from nothing. Like the garden in Bologna, this was not a metamorphosis, but was a creation that did not exist before. This, Antonio believes, is the most powerful sensation a man can have: "It makes you feel that you can do anything."

In 'Bluebois', within a carpet of cherry stones, he immersed a series of square modules holding water or blue flowers, such as meconopsis. There are similarities with Kate Cullity's 'Desert Space', though significantly that is part of her home garden, a far cry from Antonio's. At Métis, Antonio was given the freedom to choose the site and the theme. His idea was that in Quebec, where the landscape is large and you lose a sense of scale, he would design gardens (representing the proximity and importance of water in Quebec) that were variations on one square metre.

For the Giardini in Fiera Exhibition in Florence, Antonio created 'Assenzio Volatile', a garden of wild wormwood with silver Moroseta chickens (that his mother keeps and loves). The space is enclosed with a bamboo fence, giving a cage-like appearance, yet is open to weeds and wild plants generated by seeds that fly in spontaneously. The garden looks simple but is also beautiful and highly unusual for a show garden.

All Antonio's gardens are expressions of himself, but his own, naturally, does this best. He describes his garden as "something similar to a personal library, where you collect the books that you love. I have plants that perhaps do not grow well, but they remind me of places where I have loved to travel or to work. I like plants that I received from people in different circumstances and I enjoy giving plants as presents." A library is the record of a person's reading through their lives, and Antonio's garden, too, is a record of his experiences. He has frustrations due to the climate, so whereas he gets enduring pleasure from the physical nature of books, some of his plants do not survive as long. He explains, "Plants come and go and are capricious, like people. They have their own personalities. You have the same sense as when you fall in love with a beautiful woman, and something goes wrong. Then you say, 'I don't want to see you anymore. If you don't love me, leave me!' I have these feelings; I am very anthropomorphic about plants."

OPPOSITE: What looks like sand is cherry stones! Squares of reflective water and blue-flowered plants create a magical space within a wood in Quebec.

Antonio peeks out from the giant, prehistoric-looking leaves of gunnera in a damp part of his garden.

BELOW: Spontaneous plants do not care about barriers – in Perazzi's view they add beauty to gardens and enhance integration with the environment. Many, such as nettles, are also edible. Here in an exhibition garden, magenta *Amaranthus caudatus* (most parts of which can be eaten) and grasses mimic the wonderfully feathered chickens.

TONY **SMITH**

Tony Smith is a chatty, charismatic, quirky perfectionist who is refreshingly open and honest. He is best known for his innovative (sometimes controversial) conceptual gardens at events such as the Chelsea and Hampton Court Palace flower shows. Surprisingly, he does not use these as a vehicle to gain work, but as an outlet to express his creativity. His view is that there should be a total distinction between gardens to live with and ones for a show. As a result, his own garden, as well as those designed for private clients, is very different from the ones for which he is famed.

Tony established his design company, Hortus Infinitus, in 2000, and won two gold medals for conceptual gardens at Hampton Court in 2007 and 2008. He is interested in current affairs, politics and philosophy. But when asked how he gets his inspiration for his show gardens, his answer was fascinating: "I make connections that aren't normally made between different things. That is what creativity is, I think."

There is a strong similarity in this regard with music, and particularly poetry. For his 'In Digestion' garden in 2007, Tony made a connection between excesses of food and of information. A clear idea underpins each of his show gardens, and they do not rely on plants. His thought-provoking 2008 Chelsea installation, 'More Questions Than Answers', was about the Iraq war. On a black slab within a grey box, was the outline of a fallen figure in white roses, with red petals for blood. Chelsea had never had a conceptual garden category, and the fact that Tony Smith managed to bypass this, with a political installation, caused a mixture of skepticism, kudos and admiration.

'Star', at Hampton Court the same year, was an equally striking and exciting exhibit, consisting of six wheelbarrows appearing to bow toward a central plinth, on which stood a pink wheelbarrow filled with gold-sprayed coffee beans. It was a satirical comment on the Western world's obsession with fame, fashion, branding and consumption. It emphasised Tony's belief that gardens (and installations) for shows should have wow factor rather than be something from which an idea can be copied to take home. However, when I ventured to suggest that shows abroad tend to be more innovative and open-minded, he

countered by saying that at Royal Horticultural Society (RHS) shows the quality is better. Tony admits that if he looks at a conceptual garden and sees a technical flaw, he does not see anything beyond that. The finish has to be perfect in his view.

Other outstanding show gardens by Tony Smith include his 'Ecstasy in a Very Black Box', designed for MDF The BiPolar Organisation at a time when the topic was less fashionable than today. Bright, jewel-coloured, pointed Perspex shards were placed into a soft, acid-green bed, made of one million lettuce seeds, planted fourteen days prior to the show, to allow for germination and growth. These were surrounded by black tarmac and the whole was encased in a black brick wall, with slit windows, allowing the garden to be seen in sections. Tony is keen on lettuces. They have featured fabulously in two other dynamic show gardens, and he also grows them in ornamental beds in his home garden.

Quilted Velvet (the toilet paper company) approached Tony to design three gardens in 2009: at Chelsea, Hampton Court and Tatton Park. His brief was to reflect the brand and for the

'Ecstasy in a Very Black Box'. In this garden, the black wall shows the imprisonment of the mind in darker moments. Within, glimpses of bright Perspex shards, springing from a tongue of lettuce, represent ecstasy. Contrasts of texture and colour combine to raise awareness of Bipolar disorder.

OPPOSITE: 'Star'. This dramatic installation at Hampton Court sums up ideas of anti-consumerism. The gold coffee beans in the pink wheelbarrow symbolise brand name cafés and all else falsely venerated.

PREVIOUS SPREAD: In Tony's own garden, the seating area by the house is shaded by an albizia (coming into leaf in May). Though Tony loves the tree, he has not planted it in a client's garden as he is testing its hardiness and ultimate size. Ribbons of plants run through the borders, many leftover from show gardens, where their impact was entirely different.

gardens to be 12 × 10 metres, but other than that, fortunately, knowing his conceptual work, they gave him a very free hand. Tony did some research but did not write anything down. The Chelsea design had to be done in a week, and working with a graphic designer, miraculously, it was. Very often, Tony says, he will get a whole design, in his head, in minutes.

My favourite of the Quilted Velvet designs was the one at Hampton Court, which won a gold medal. The message of sustainability was clear: 30,000 tiny oak trees were incased and seemingly protected by simple but imposing structures formed of green oak. In the centre, three blue cedar trees and the trunk of a fallen tree emphasised the fact that Quilted Velvet plant three new trees for every one they chop down. The paired down palette of materials, colours and planting gave a restful, harmonious effect. The oak structures had an almost monk-like serenity. The whole was immensely atmospheric and powerful. But Tony does not mind that his show gardens are temporary and are then dismantled: he puts it behind him, having already moved on to his next idea.

His first garden sponsored by Easigrass, in 2010, attracted some disapproving comments for introducing artificial grass to an RHS flower show for the first time, but the garden was imaginative, innovative and spectacular. The idea behind it was that it belonged to an eccentric bachelor, living in the city with a high-powered job. It was an escape where he could indulge his love of plants. In front were ferns, *Tulipa* 'China Pink' with *Verbena bonariensis* and bronze fennel within a grass-covered, secluded grotto. Behind was a kitchen, filled with orchids. Interestingly, this garden was in fact quite personal, containing many elements that Tony would ideally like in his home garden, where he has, to an extent, compromised to fulfill the wishes of his family.

But when it comes to show gardens, Tony is single-minded and very competitive. His design for Chelsea 2011, which was fully sponsored, was deemed too dark and deep: it was not celebratory enough and was not accepted. Though he was hurt, he still aims to use his idea in the future. What he regrets most, long term, is that every year when he exhibited he bought a Chelsea china mug with the date on. Though he visited the show, he would not buy a mug in 2011, so his set will be incomplete and this sadly bothers him. However, his 2011 Hampton Court garden 'Diamonds and Rust', for Easigrass, was another showstopper. Green, smoking, industrial chimneys appeared amongst rolling hills. It addressed human perceptions of time, from permanent geological features to transient man-made structures. Yet again, it was received to great acclaim.

OPPOSITE ABOVE: The forest of 30,000 miniature oak trees reflect Quilted Velvet's tree planting initiatives. A line of purple heather runs through the seedlings, using the same colour as the brand. But even if one knows nothing of this, the garden is still stunning.

OPPOSITE BELOW: This garden had a magical feeling as though one had just stepped into a fabulous forest glade, although it is actually highly symmetrical.

BELOW: "No matter how hard I try, I can see no clear dividing line between garden design and art", says Tony Smith. This 2011 garden, 'Diamonds and Rust', at Hampton Court exemplifies this theory.

ABOVE: Stepping-stones, over water strewn with lily pads, lead into this atomospheric building.

BELOW: Tony loves ruins and unfinished buildings (his ideal project would be to create a garden at Tintern Abbey). Meanwhile, this structure he built, with bare rafters above, creates wonderful reflections in the water below.

OPPOSITE: A highly unusual combination that works brilliantly: lettuces and ferns. But Tony plans to replace the lettuces with epimediums. He claims, endearingly, "I am determined that one day I will grow up and be ordinary. I think my wife might prefer it."

Tony's success is the more remarkable because he is self-taught and came into garden design relatively late. He finds it difficult to study, or remember facts that do not interest him. When Tony was five, he would take bits of coal out of the bunker, or coins out of his money box and plant them in the garden hoping they might grow. For fifteen years afterwards, whenever he dug his parents' garden, he would find old pennies and bits of coal. When he was nine, his parents had an allotment that he helped with. But when he was eleven, he started playing tennis, and by the time he was a teenager he was competing for Surrey and took part in the qualifiers for Wimbledon. Yet when he left school at sixteen, his report from the headmaster said, 'Anthony will never amount to anything'. Tony admits he was disruptive at school, but he has certainly proved his headmaster wrong.

Tony became a tennis coach and also helped the groundsman and did a bit of gardening. After about fifteen years, when Tony was married with two small boys, a lady whose garden he had looked after died and she left him some money. This allowed him to stop tennis coaching and start gardening and designing; his clients from the tennis club became customers, while he also became interested in improving school grounds.

In 2004, Tony created a school garden at Hampton Court, similar to an amphitheatre, or outdoor classroom, and once the show was over, he rebuilt it at his sons' school for no charge. He thought his sons would benefit from this, but a year later he moved. However, he did get lots of commissions from other schools. Tony and his family moved to a house built in 2001, in West Sussex. He bought it because, despite being situated on the edge of a town, it has open views of fields to the side and the house is very light inside. The garden originally consisted of a lawn sloping down to the bottom, a shed, and the existing maple, magnolia, cedar and eucalyptus trees. After Tony had lived here about two weeks, he got rid of the shed and marked the outline of the present garden on the ground. It has evolved to an extent since, but basically the structure is the same.

The garden flows in colourful swirls from the house, and is filled with memories, obsessions and a sense of fun. Before I arrived, Tony had mown the central lawn in perfect, curving stripes. He apologised for the rabbit hutch in the middle, but this is very much a family garden. His wife, Karen, insists on having sweet peas every year. Tony's greenhouse, in which he had hoped to grow orchids (as in his Chelsea show garden), is filled with cacti and succulents that his two sons like. Many of these were grown from cuttings; one was taken from Brighton sea front; some were given to the children by their grandparents; one grew from a seed that his son sowed when he was three. Tony's idea for a fernery – a cool hideaway for him to sit in – was scuppered when his sons desperately wanted Koi Carp. The result is a fabulous, ruin-like building, with a floor dug out 1.5 metres deep, an open roof and windows in rippling walls with water running into the still pool where the carp live. The ferns now grow outside, so Tony still has "a modest, slightly beleaguered collection of ferns, some left over from the Chelsea Easigrass garden".

Tony's home garden, approximately 30 metres by 14 metres, is not divided into 'rooms', but is an open space, with varied atmospheres and plants of different character in sun or shade. Your eye is drawn along the curves, in a long route that makes the garden seem bigger. One of the reasons why this garden is seen as a whole is that Tony, intriguingly, dislikes things that are added on. For this reason he loathes extensions to houses and hates estate cars, because he sees them as a car with a bit on the back. He can't stand roof racks, even though it would be useful to have one for his work. Though he claims to like other gardens that are divided into rooms, he prefers to design those where space changes through movement. A small change in level or a bend alters the view as you move. As Tony admits, "I like solidity but get bored very quickly."

Tony is very conscious of the importance of transitions, especially in hard landscaping. He built many of the walls in his own garden himself. This has also led to touches of individuality. Tony's tortoise, which he found on his parents' allotment when he was ten, is still alive and happy in his garden. She has free reign, grazing on dandelions that Tony leaves growing for her. He also built a tiny wall, largely concealed, but requiring six or seven tons of stone, all round the garden purely to keep the tortoise from escaping.

Many of the wide variety of plants have a personal history: some were given by friends (such as a miniature myrtle given by Cleve West); others are leftovers from shows (verbena and bronze fennel from Chelsea, heather from Hampton Court); while some have been collected on holidays. Others are grown for their scent, for example the evergreen, fragrant-flowered, Chilean *Azara microphylla*. In spring, Tony tells me, the whole garden is perfumed with vanilla from the tiny flowers that appear in the leaf axels.

Tony also likes bedding and is happy to incorporate it into the scheme. For example, he has found that tuberous rooted begonias are hardy, and in his late summer border he grows yellow, pink and red ones that have survived the coldest winter. The red ones were brought back from the chimneys in his 2011 garden at Hampton Court. His comment is: "It's not particularly tasteful, but it's fun." Also light-hearted, and to my mind glorious, is his unusual planting of lettuces alongside ferns, beneath a cedar, in a wonderful combination of colour and texture.

On the other side of the cedar Tony has started a bed of cyclamen, inspired by the rockery at Wisley, which he says makes him tingle each time he sees it. He is now really excited that both his *Cyclamen hederifolium* and *C. coum* are self-seeding and he has a vision of the area completely carpeted in these delicate pink, swan-like flowers. It will create a surprise that would not be visible from the rest of the garden. The planting is always changing. As Tony explains, "Part of me wants a pristine, perfect garden, and part wants something different, so almost before one thing has fulfilled itself, another is on the go. I almost need two gardens, one with everything just so, and another next door to play in. To some extent the garden is a hotchpotch because of that, but since there are reasonably strong bones underneath, I hope it hangs together."

Walking back towards the house from the bottom of the garden is a beautiful *Eucryphilla nymanensis*, a small tree that Tony maintains he could not be without. The sweetly scented flowers have four creamy-white petals with a spray of stamens in the centre that sparkle in the sun. This variety is more hardy than most, but it still suffers some damage in severe winters. Further up is a bed of exotic, later-flowering plants, such as hedychium, tall explosions of half-hardy ricinus (castor oil plant), bananas as well as self-seeded nasturtiums.

Tony says he would not create this for a client, because he would be more disciplined, and would also design something requiring less maintenance (unless he knew that the client had a gardener). Moreover his own garden is very personal. "The steps are all made my size", Tony tells me, as I gaze up at his lofty height, "because I get fed up having to make everything smaller for everyone else. I am also a bit of a collector, although that is less of a problem than it used to be. If I had one trachycarpus, I needed to have all six species, but I have got over that now."

Calendula mingle with nasturtium in a picture of yellow. Both flowers are self-sown favourites. If Tony sees interesting variations of calendula, be they more lemony or more orange, he will take a few seeds from wherever he finds them.

OPPOSITE ABOVE: Vibrant combinations abound in this garden. Here black, velvety aeoniums partner blue agapanthus and scarlet crocosmia. Airy height is provided by purple *Verbena bonariensis* and bronze fennel.

OPPOSITE BELOW: Tony considers his garden as he sits on a wall he built. Behind him is a typical bed of plants of wonderfully varied texture and colour.

Although, actually, he does have rather a lot of cordylines grown from different batches of seed from various suppliers, to try to find hardier ones, not really for clients, but for himself. One cordyline, Tony feels, can change the whole atmosphere of a place. He first got interested in cordylines 20 years ago, when he noticed a bedding scheme on a roundabout near where he lived. The cordylines were not removed in winter and many came through. But he would not plant them in a client's garden because he cannot guarantee their hardiness.

Tony believes that the Arts and Crafts style is the pinnacle of what is nice to live with in a garden. His own plot has strong structure, uses natural materials and planting that is slightly more formal towards the house, becoming less so. Near the house he mixes annuals, perennials, natives and exotics (such as aeoniums and bananas) in bold colour combinations (yellow and purple is a favourite). He also has, for example, one red and three orange azaleas sharing a corner, because, "although Karen says it clashes, I like it being exciting. Shape, form, proportion, scale, I feel comfortable with, but colour always surprises me."

Tony also enjoys a combination of the naturalistic and effortless with some drama, or theatricality. He makes an analogy with professional photographers, who place models in funky, extravagant outfits against backgrounds of derelict or ruined buildings. In his

own garden, this is achieved with the building that houses the pond. For one of his clients, he created a derelict potting shed out of the remains of outbuildings already in the garden. Tony's clients tend to be fairly local people, who have been recommended by word of mouth. They are mostly without enormous budgets, and his gardens for them are practical as well as naturalistic, and plant- and site-orientated, in a style not dissimilar from that in his own.

His briefs, while often requesting impact and year-round colour also usually call for low maintenance. He explains that many people think of their outdoor space in a similar way to their living room. They think they can do the room up and it will be finished. But because Tony's clients have mainly seen other gardens he has designed for their friends, he does not have too many problems. Tony also still designs a lot of imaginative school gardens. He explains that once you have done Chelsea, people tend to assume your designs will be expensive, but he enjoys creating down-to-earth gardens that are nevertheless sensitive and built with care and attention.

The shows, the school gardens and the ones for private clients are all separate in Tony's mind, as is his own garden. But his approach to each one is fairly similar. He describes it as an artistic response to certain input, plus something a bit quirky because he cannot help it. He likens it more to an artistic outpouring than designing, and considers himself a creator rather than a designer. As he puts it, "A designer plans a garden; I don't plan them." He goes on to say, "I think Tom Stuart-Smith, though I am not in his league, works the same way, because that is how you get atmosphere. Carefully planned gardens, that just fit in elements that the client wants, such as a hot tub, or a pond, are often soulless." Tony acknowledges that what he does requires time spent detailing and, if the garden is private, you have to make sure that everything is practical. But he believes he has been lucky to be able to create. He would really like to do more artistic installations.

Tony admits that his own garden is partly a chore: a busman's holiday. He does all the gardening himself, because he would not trust anyone else with it, and it is sometimes a strain to keep up. Nevertheless, he says that in order to be creative, to understand planting conditions, and fulfill the wishes of your client, you need to have lived with a large proportion of the plants you specify. It is also important to Tony that the garden makes the best of the house. His is a space in which the house sits well and is comfortable for the family. It is also a place where he can experiment freely: he talks of it as his playground. While Tony's show gardens express his imagination, his own garden expresses his personality. As he says, "It's whole and in bits all at once. It's calm and restless as well. Contradictory."

TED **SMYTH**

Ted Smyth's own garden is the antithesis of those he creates for clients. It is not minimalist, innovative, sophisticated and chic, but is luxuriant, comfortable, intimate and eclectic. It is beautiful, but completely in keeping with Ted's individuality and his outspoken, down-to-earth, slightly Bohemian personality.

This 1.6-hectare garden, outside Auckland, New Zealand, includes two small hills and a valley, and surrounds the house where Ted has lived for the past 40 years. The location, in the foothills of a Bush park, is semi-rural, although, being on a corner site, there are roads on two sides of the house with neighbours on one side. However, as Ted puts it, "I have planted the neighbours out really heavily so I don't have to see them." He continues: "I built my house myself, and because I didn't have much money, I used a lot of demolition material." The walls are wood and the roof is metal but there are more windows than wall.

Today's house and garden are far removed from the scene that greeted Ted when he first arrived. Then there were one-and-a-half falling down rooms – part of an 1830s cottage that was actually moved from Auckland to the present site. Instead of the garden, there was a tip of rubbish and abandoned cars. The

soil was west Auckland clay. Ted chose the place simply because "it was real cheap and I could see it had potential". At that time, with a new partner, who had young children, Ted made a large lawn for his stepdaughters to play on and a small swimming pool for his second family.

Ted left his previous house (also built of demolition material) to start again. He says that he did not have a plan for the garden, but that it has evolved, piecemeal. He distinguishes very clearly between this and what he calls 'my job'. Those gardens, Ted says, "are very planned. Because I am a self-taught architect, they include a lot of three-dimensional construction work; there is a much more architectural quality to my work gardens. This one, where I live, is deliberately the opposite."

PREVIOUS SPREAD: A sculpture in Ted's garden adds impact to a multi-surfaced path, flanked by fronds of every variety.

ABOVE: A favourite stone on which Ted can sit amidst his plants, contemplating the pond.

OPPOSITE: This view, showing the shade house, with its spectral light and shadows, exemplifies the Gauguinesque, jungle feel of Ted's garden.

Ted's own garden, reached through the house, has an ordinary pool, "nothing like that highly developed designer stuff that I do for a living", and then the garden slopes downwards. Unlike his commissioned work, here, spaces are not clearly divided; there are no strongly defining lines, but a homogonous whole. A brick path runs between two fishponds, about which Ted comments, with his wry, dry sense of humour: "All that cottagey stuff, again, totally different from my work gardens. Water in my work gardens is always clear and treated, but this is all very unsophisticated. I don't think there is a path in my own garden that I have ever finished, for some reason, whether it is brick or exposed pebble agrogate or tracks with a bit of shell in them. They are just whatever took my fancy at the time. But it is all very down-market."

His planting, too, is more naturalistic and much denser than for clients, displaying his passion for subtropical specimens. Ted uses some of these in his commissioned gardens, but genereally more natives. As he admits with typical frankness, "I don't have any interest in mowing lawns and all that kind of nonsense, so once the children grew up, I planted the whole place. I have got a *thing* about palms, cycads and bromeliads." His favourite palm is the butia (from areas of Brazil, Uruguay and Argentina), with strongly arching, elliptic leaves. Architectural shape and texture are paramount. Palms with very feathery leaves are dismissed by Ted as being "a bit hula"; he prefers fan shapes. Most New Zealand natives, Ted explains, grow too big for his garden, though he does love *Rhopalostylis sapida* (Nikau palm), with its stout, single green trunk (up to about 12 metres) topped by fronds, held in a smooth bulging crownshaft. Ted rates the 'Chatham Island' form especially highly.

Ted's advice is to always try to visualise the eventual size of a tree you are planting, however small it may appear initially. His garden is full, but nothing overpowers. Paths weave through a jungle landscape filled with fronds in different shades of green. 'Fingers' fan, point, arc and whorl in all directions. Palms include *Livistonia chinesis* (Chinese fan palm), *Butia capitata* (Jelly palm), with its slender, blue-grey leaves, and *Brahea armata* (Grey goddess palm). There is also the palm-like encephalartos, with its short stem and pinnate, hard, leathery, spiny leaves. Nearer the ground, the central purple bract of *Neoregelia concentrica* glows amid dense rosettes of glossy, green leaves. In the canopy above, the long stalked, mid-green, lance-shaped leaves of *Howea forsteriana,* are borne almost horizontally, with pendant tips. Later these will bear ellipsoid, orange-red fruit. There are jewels of colour but a predominance of green. Ted asserts, "I don't like all those plants that have got yellow and spots and stripes all over them."

Ted has gradually fallen in love with hardy subtropical plants and filled his garden with them. He says, "I like to live with a garden all around me, not that I necessarily go out and *stroke* it every five minutes! But I couldn't live in one of those suburban horror places." Now Ted does not do all the gardening himself, nor does he have the energy or time to change the garden a great deal, though he still enjoys it. But if someone else had made it, he says, he would not be in the least bit interested in it. "Even my wife doesn't interfere in it", he adds.

Ted's personal plot is very much based around planting, rather than structure, because, he says, he can afford plants. Mostly, he planted small specimens that have grown. His commissioned work relies far more on hard landscaping, and what Ted calls "simplicity and clarity". His own garden does, however, include a few decorative pieces. Beside the pond is a sculpture made by Ted's stepson. A skeletal boat, raised on leaf-like stilts, rises from the water – its ribbed sides echoing the strappy leaves by its side (see p.162). There are also unusual urns, in fact old crucibles for smelting metal. These are used by Ted in some of his clients' gardens, as planters. In his own garden they are purely ornamental. "They are rather beautiful" he says, "but there is nothing in them except water and bloody mosquitoes!" Another signature feature of Ted's garden is the inclusion of large, smooth stones, which seem Japanese in influence.

A substantial paper was written about Ted in 2005, entitled *Celebrating Ted Smyth: The Emergence of Modern Space in New Zealand Gardens*. It states: 'This paper examines the influence of Japanese gardens on the work of Ted Smyth, arguably New Zealand's most influential landscape architect.' However Ted denies this influence, claiming, "I got a little bit involved in Japanese gardens when I first started, for a very short period of time, because that was all I knew. I had a book about them. But I soon realised that kind of stuff was nothing to do with me. By about 1965 I had definitely developed my own vocabulary. Up until the '90s I was obsessed by what I call the *contemporary*, not Modernism, which is too generalised. Since then the poetic has become my consuming obsession: landscape as poetry. At the same time it is totally contemporary." Ted continues,

OPPOSITE ABOVE LEFT: Beautiful *Brahea armata* is reputed to have the bluest leaves of any palm and is drought and frost resisitant.

OPPOSITE ABOVE RIGHT: The jagged lime-green fans of *Trachycarpus fortunei* or Chusan palm. Though native to China, this palm will grow in most parts of Britain.

OPPOSITE BELOW: *Aloe plicatilis*, from South Africa, has smooth, grey leaves, tinged pink, like a multi-fingered, giant, outstretched hand.

"There are dozens of imitators of my work in New Zealand, and some of them don't do too bad a job, but I try never to stay still; I am always progressing, so they can't keep up!"

Ted is still working and attracting plaudits from around the world. Though untrained in horticulture, architecture, or landscape design, his acquired knowledge stretches back over 50 years. Born in Auckland in 1937, he trained as a graphic artist and began painting and exhibiting in the 1960s. To make a bit more money, he started designing and building gardens, and developed a landscape practice, Ted Smyth and Associates. During the '70s and '80s he developed his signature style. Ted is now New Zealand's most highly respected landscape architect, with work ranging from design with an intense, inventive sculptural content to native restoration projects, and from private gardens to public parks. He is fêted for the pared back

Ted designed this garden for a private client. Shallow steps lead into the swimming pool that appears to merge with Auckland Harbour. The island in the background is Rangitoto, a volcano regarded as iconic by New Zealanders.

OPPOSITE: A dramatic contemporary sculpture by Rudi Van der Pol appears to float above the lily pond in Ted's garden.

elegance of his designs, complemented by his subtle use of subtropical and native plants.

In particular, Ted is noted for some spectacular private gardens built in Auckland, often located on cliff-top sites, focusing on an infinity swimming pool. These pools, which became popular in the 1990s, produce the visual effect of extending into the sea or the horizon; the far edge vanishes, or blends with infinity. They are very expensive, requiring extensive and complex structural and hydraulic engineering, as well as architectural detailing.

Smyth was the first person to introduce infinity pools to New Zealand. As he says, "I work on some very expensive sites and a lot of them are coastal. I couldn't afford to live on the coast, but I work for some very wealthy people." With the pools often came marble tiles, and two of his favourite materials, stainless steel and neon. Ted explains, "Stainless steel doesn't have a lot of flashy personality; unlike brass and copper, it's lean and it's mean. It can be really sculptural, without imposing materialism."

When Ted was a painter, he did a series of rainbows, which were very geometric: some vertical, some horizontal, but all were formalised strips of colour. It was, he maintains, only a small jump from those paintings to using neon as an abstract and controlled material in his commissioned gardens. For example, he might have a large stainless steel portal that frames a view, with perhaps a blue neon light edging it. It is a device that brings the outer landscape into the garden, while at the same time projecting the garden outwards.

Ted has developed an aesthetic that emphasises the arrangements of garden elements in space, and reveals his fascination with the relationship between organic and mineral surfaces. This is also evident in the major public spaces he has designed in Auckland and Tauranga. As he says, "I still believe that landscaping is an art form. I used to say that a lot, and everyone thought I was nuts, but now everyone and his uncle wants to be a landscape artist, so I don't talk about it anymore."

His artistry, and his place in contemporary landscape tradition, is seen in his dominant use of structure without an axis; restricted ornamentation; material diversity; and use of sculptural plants. Following in the footsteps of the British landscape architect, Geoffrey Jellicoe (1900–1966), Ted may insist on the role of the designer as form-giver, but his influence is undeniable, and the more remarkable because he is self-taught. Ted considers himself an excellent plantsman, too, as well he should. His commissioned gardens are not reliant on flowers, but trees and plants that he brought into prominence because of their sculptural qualities; these are now readily available and widely used. Notwithstanding, an amazing, cave-like courtyard garden that Ted designed for one client has no plants at all, relying entirely upon stainless steel, neon and water.

Of all Ted's work, he considers Quay Park (covering 0.8 hectares within a new city development in Auckland) to be

seminal. He claims, "It combines a huge amount of poetic material along with Maori material. The poetic is the allusion to what it is all about: the sea, because Quay Park is on reclaimed land. So I was working with the poetry of the site and the sea, as well as the fact that it is owned by Ngati Whatua, a local pre-eminent tribe in Auckland."

As a result, the pavement – a glorious pattern of texture and colour – incorporates various forms of Koru, a spiral Maori symbol representing the fern frond, also associated with family and the tribe. Ted was aware that certain sacred symbols

should not be put on the ground or sat on, because that is desecration, so the symbols he used were modernised and abstracted. There is a large sculpture designed by Ted, made of stainless steel, which refers to the Koru. Some seats evoke Maori geometry, others waves: displaying the versatility of precast concrete, they wriggle their way through the site.

Because Ted's home garden is so very different from the ones he designs for clients, I asked, "If money was not a factor, would you prefer to own one of your commissioned gardens, or the garden you have?" This was his reply: "That is a question I have asked myself many times and, to be honest, I think I am more comfortable with what I've got. I am not sure that I want to live in one of my *planned* gardens. I have a beard because I hate having to shave every day. That is how I like to live. I think I would look a bit *funny* in one of my *real* gardens."

Architectural elements dominate Quay Park, from stainless steel nets above, to wave-like benches below. A pool, based on the three-fingered hand, is just one of the many Maori symbols; others are found in the finely patterned concrete paths.

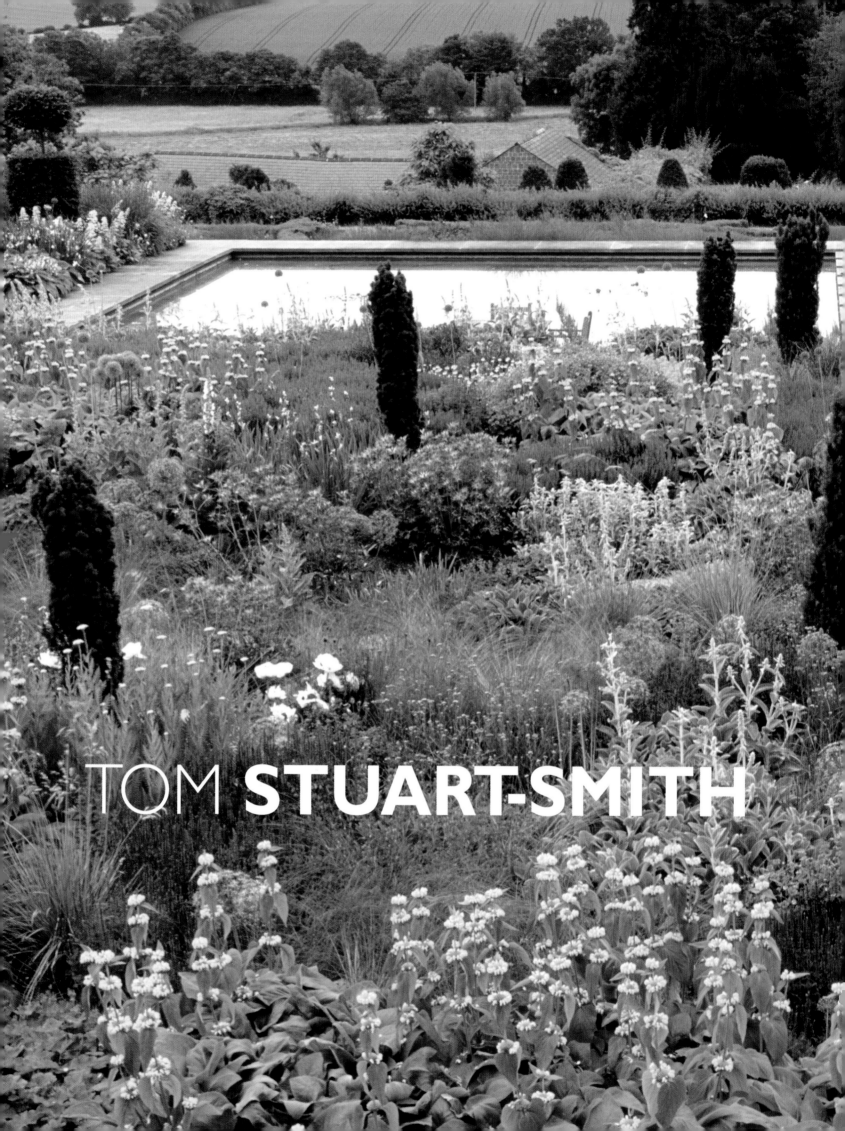

TOM **STUART-SMITH**

When I think of Tom Stuart-Smith's work, I think of gardens seamlessly merging with their surroundings; mounds of profuse perennials and graceful grasses interspersed with tall topiary; and jewel-like irises in golden grasses beside rusted steel tanks brimful with still water. All this, including the last – an enduring memory of his 2006 Chelsea garden – can be enjoyed and admired in Tom's home garden, Serge Hill Barn, in Hertfordshire.

Tom Stuart-Smith has won seven gold medals at Chelsea, including three Best in Show, and has gained an international reputation for his ability to combine naturalism and modernity. His landscapes are elegant and uncluttered though not minimal, and his trademark planting is inspired by meadows and prairies. Juxtaposition and contrast is a theme that runs through much of his work, with the aim to create places of imaginative possibility.

With busy parents, who gave him encouragement and freedom, Tom started gardening when he was about fifteen. He spent most of his pocket money on plants and learnt by trial and error. After reading Landscape Design at Manchester University, he worked for various designers and for the Royal Horticultural Society, setting up his own practice in 1998. His work includes large gardens and parks open to the public (such as the Queen's Jubilee Garden at Windsor Castle and the planting around the glasshouse at the RHS's flagship garden at Wisley), private gardens (such as the stunning Broughton Grange in Oxfordshire, see pp.166-7), and the restoration of historic gardens (such as Trentham in Staffordshire, England's largest formal garden).

It is significant that Tom, though eloquent and thoughtful, is vague about the size of his own garden, since it is difficult to know where it ends and the countryside begins, but it is about one hectare. The garden surrounds a beautiful seventeenth-century, timber-framed barn, next door to Tom's parents' house, where he and his brother grew up, amid 100 hectares of rural land, albeit now on the verges of the M1 and M25. The

Left: This composition in spring green shows the strong structure of the garden and its layers of texture. Soft grass gives way to cloud-pruned yew, low box, and blocks of hornbeam. Vertical accents are provided by fastigiate yew, echoed by poplars behind.

Above: Rolo, the dachshund, spurns tiptoeing through the tulips in favour of running through the narcissi (pheasant's eye), naturalised in the grass in front of the black-painted barn.

Previous spread: At Broughton Grange, reflective water frames a fabulous tapestry of planting, punctuated by topiary mimicking the shapes of the countryside. Even the rounded phlomis in the foreground repeats the contour of the hills, which seem part of this garden.

barn was converted into a spectacular, though modestly sized house by Tom's father, a year after Tom married Sue in 1986. At that time there was no garden, just exposed stony ground. Influenced by Arts and Crafts gardens such as Sissinghurst and Hidcote, Tom began by creating a series of hedged enclosures around the barn. Using yew and hornbeam – emulating the mixed hazel, holly and hornbeam hedges in the landscape – he created defined spaces that are smaller and more intensely planted nearest the barn.

In his book, *The Barn Garden*, Tom writes that this plot, on the edge of his childhood territory, has been the most engrossing project of his gardening life: 'Over nearly quarter of a century it has shaped my opinions about making gardens more than any other place... Making a garden for yourself is very different from doing it for somebody else. So much of the pleasure is to do with the coaxing and tending, the daily observance of small details and the accumulation of change over the years.'

Over time, the land Tom owns and has incorporated into his garden has grown and changed, organically. He and Sue have three children who had climbing frames, a trampoline and sandpit within the garden. The children have now moved out and the garden has also become freer: there are fewer hedges than there used to be – the courtyard, for instance, was originally filled with box hedges, roses and vegetables.

Now Tom's garden has a mixture of geometry and naturalism; it is disciplined in terms of whether planting is contained or not; and it has spatial variety. In the main, west garden, a central strip of green grass carpet stretches from a paved dining area by the house, out into woodland. On the way it bissects deep herbaceous borders, rises up two steps and along more borders with fastigiate yews, into a surprise, serene, rectangular lawn surrounded by hornbeam hedges. As Tom discloses, "I think it often works to have the middle of the garden empty." Here another axis crosses the lawn: a hornbeam circle on the south side and to the north, a smaller rectangular lawn edged in hornbeam, ending with a view of meadow.

Both axes connect an enclosed refuge with the landscape beyond. To Tom, a garden is about reflection and contemplation and if one has too much action throughout it is too overpowering. As he points out, "Gardens need to find resolution somewhere. Some are able to find it in the landscape. But this garden's relation with the landscape is quite hermetic; it is to do with peeping out, so it is important to have a quiet centre." Tom does not like dictating set routes in any of his gardens and here views open up diagonally, enticing the eye, while glimpses of planting lure the foot this way and that.

The borders wow with their rampant diversity and drama. Tom's planting in his own garden is similar to that in his commissioned work, though with a few indulgencies. He admits to growing some plants, such as echinaceas, which do not do very well in his dry soil, just because he likes them. But increasingly, he is trying to steer the garden towards plants that are really happy and do not require much looking after. This poses the risk that they take over. "I think there are intrinsic problems with my own garden to do with plants that I really like, but which are very unruly. Near the barn, *Hesperis matronalis* var. *albiflora* provides a glorious, scented froth of white in summer, but it is such a vigorous self-seeder that I pull out trailer-loads of it every year and would never plant hesperis in a commissioned garden", he says. Another plant he would rarely use elsewhere is *Allium aflatunense*, unless he first warned the client to rigorously deadhead it once flowering was over, since it can spread everywhere. "I have quite a lot of plants that misbehave, but are beautiful, like verbascums and opium poppies. I try to make gardens for other people that are relatively stable, and then if they have a good gardener, they can start introducing the randomising element."

Formality in Tom's garden is softened by the fine, naturalistic planting for which he is acclaimed. While the strong structure and plentiful planting might be said to be Arts and Crafts style,

BELOW: Embracing the extended landscape is typical of Tom Stuart-Smith's designs. Here a gap in the yew hedge gives a framed glimpse of the meadow and fields beyond.

OPPOSITE: South of the main axis, the garden is less ordered, in spring displaying bountiful drifts of white narcissi: 'Thalia', 'WP Milner' and 'Jenny'.

Tom counters this, saying, "If a garden is nostalgic, I would want to juxtapose it with something quite modern. I think places that are tremendously nostalgic, like Hidcote, are wonderful, but I would never want to make something like that myself; it feels like a historic garden." Nostalgia, Tom explains, implies not only looking back, but also a sense of loss. He is more interested in what is happening now. One of the things that makes Tom's gardens outstanding as well as modern is his use of grasses – in his own garden, they make up around 20 per cent of the planting. Seeing Thijssepark near Amsterdam in the 1980s, and knowing and collaborating with Piet Oudolf (master of the prairie planting style) were key to him.

Tom is associated with interweaving swathes of voluptuous plants such as achillea, astrantia, campanula, cardoons, cranesbill, eryngium, euphorbia, miscanthus, nepeta, phlox, salvia and stipa.

He maintains, however, that texture is more important to him than colour, admitting, "I wouldn't say I was an enormously subtle plantsman, like, say, Dan Pearson, who seems to have studied every plant combination in terms of how things inter-react. I tend to use a broader brush." Tom claims he is no longer interested in growing a huge range of specimen plants but is keener to think more about an overall pallet and the atmoshpere that he is trying to create. He thinks more in terms of textural juxtapositions, rhythm and repetition, than whether one colour will look good next to another. He does not, however, use orange or bright red flowers much, unless it is in very small spaces, because he feels they have an ability to detract from other plants.

I visited Tom's garden in spring, when there was a lovely delicacy: an intake of breath before the full flood of floriferous summer. The meadow was sprinkled with cowslips and pheasants eyes; curved beds held white Narcissus 'Thalia'; and the promising, burgeoning shoots of herbaceous plants were spot lit against the wavy folds of yew 'curtains'. The central, filigree hornbeam 'screens' appeared light enough to be picked up and moved, like stage flats, to change the scene.

The enclosed courtyard garden at the front of the house, partially transposed from Chelsea 2006, was filled not with irises, as then, but tulips. It is unusual for a Chelsea designer to take most of their garden home. In Tom's case, it was the idea of his wife, Sue. She (like thousands of others) was captivated by the intense colours of the planting and the warm rust of the Corten steel tanks of Tom's 2006 garden. When it was unsold at the end of the show, and the steel structures were due to be dismantled and transported to the contractor's yard, she saw a wonderful opportunity.

Tom has not incorporated all the structures or all of the planting into his own garden, but the modernism without minimalism, which was the central concept for Chelsea, as well as the contrasts between a simple, linear plan with planting of complex texture and colour, remains. Moreover it is appropriate here, for although the Corten is a modern material, it recalls the rusty farm machinery of the former farmyard, while the glowing planting looks wonderful against the traditional black-painted wooden barn.

This garden is far more open than it was in Chelsea, without the rills and trees, but with brick paths echoing the orange clay roof tiles of the barn and seductive, simple, black sun loungers beside a rusted Corten wall. In summer, some of the planting around the raised ponds brimming with water is the same as it was at Chelsea: rich, coppery bearded irises 'Attention please', 'Supreme Sultan' and 'Vintage Wine', amongst drifts of burgundy *Astrantia* 'Ruby Wedding', and translucent grasses *Hakonechloa macra* and *Anemanthele lessoniana*. But to increase seasonal interest, snowdrops have also been planted here, succeeded by dwarf narcissi and then brilliant tulips.

The courtyard is an area for relaxing at the centre of the house, continuously viewed through the large glass windows, but most of Tom's plot is used for gardening. When I arrived, Tom was meticulously spot-treating his newly planted wild flower meadow with weed killer, having found the tiny leaves of unwanted buttercup emerging. He had started at 6.30 a.m. and is happy to weed all day. Sue was working in the new greenhouse, beside the vegetable garden. This area is a joyous surprise, where raised beds are edged with multi-coloured

tulips and anemones: bright necklaces around the spring-bare earth. In a reversal of the stereotype where the man tends vegetables and the woman grows flowers, this kitchen garden is Sue's domain. They also employ one full-time and one part-time gardener. But as Tom says, "Some people might do yoga; I do gardening. It is a kind of meditation. I work very hard at my job, and the garden is the one thing that enables me to stop and take time out. It is very important to me and if I don't get time in the garden my pressure levels go up."

OPPOSITE: In the courtyard, still water in the Corten tanks gives glorious reflections. In the foreground, Tulipa 'Gavota' glows.

BELOW: The texture and colour of the materials and planting in this Chelsea garden were unforgettable. *Viburnum rhytidophyllum* is pruned to display its angular branches against the rusted steel walls; viburnum is not incorporated in Tom's home courtyard, though the essence of this garden is retained.

It is clear that Tom's garden means a huge amount to him. His commissioned gardens, several of which are open to the public, enable others to appreciate his work. A favourite is Broughton Grange in Oxfordshire (see pp. 166-7). Though it has a strong formal structure, it was clearly conceived entirely in relation to the surrounding landscape, with views to distant clumps of trees, hills, valleys and vistas. This backdrop merges with the garden, while its undulating shapes are echoed in the planting. Three south-facing terraces on different levels hold tapestries of closely planted flowers and grasses. An imposing, modern, stone rill carries water down to a large stone tank, which appears to float between the garden and the horizon. It seems the perfect design to fit this enclosed 60-metre square space that used to be a paddock.

In a recent BBC interview, Tom was asked, "If you could design a garden for anyone, who would it be and why?" His intriguing reply was, "Somebody who wasn't interested in gardening but was interested in the idea of what a garden could mean." I asked him to elaborate on this, and he told me that he really liked working for people who are interested in the debate about the essentials of a place and why one would want to do certain things, rather than how one would do them. He admitted, "If I work for somebody who starts cross examining me about iris varieties, or asking me why I am using a particular plant, I would switch off pretty rapidly, because I just think that I know how to do it."

Tom is happy if people tell him they do not like grasses very much and want the quantity reduced, or if they say they hate a certain colour. He recalls, "I once worked for a divorcee who said, 'I can't bear yellow because it is the colour of cuckoldry and every time I see it, it reminds me of being deceived by my husband.' I was fine with omitting yellow from her garden, but if I do a considered planting plan for someone, and they start questioning it, I feel: that is how I paint, it is what I do; it is the only time that I would ever get irritated with someone." Tom goes on to explain that he feels it is absolutely the client's prerogative to say, for example, that they are someone who likes enclosure and needs to have some small spaces around him or her, before opening the space up to the landscape. That kind of debate, about how people feel about space and how they want to use it, and their perceptions of what a garden could mean, Tom relishes, regretting it if a client merely declares that they want the garden to look beautiful.

So what does Tom's own garden mean to him? "If you are being pompous," he replies, "it represents a worldview. It is a lot of who I am and what I believe in. It is about the degree of privacy and openness to the outside world, which is why a lot of it is quite internalised, but actually it has very distinct and clear openings in the way that it brings landscape in – even though perhaps not as much as in my commissioned work. It is about variety versus monoculture. You could say it is about contrast, but it is also about the essential dialectical quality of life, of opposing tendencies, which you spend your life trying to resolve and you make a better or worse fist of it depending on who you are and how you live. That in its most obvious way is expressed in terms of the contrast of order and disorder, but the garden is a constant interplay of contrasts, perhaps again, not as much as some of my other gardens that may have a very strong tension between imposed order and a more subversive feel. It is about order overlaid or interwoven, and the whole coming together to make a coherent picture.

"And for me, it is about gardening and the culture of a place; making it come into being and looking after it. That has been very important to us. We moved here with one tiny child, six months old, and we brought our three children up here, and as they have grown the garden has grown around them. It is all about a nurturing custodianship rather than ownership and possession. I am too young to think about what happens after Sue and I leave here or die, but I don't really mind. I think the most important thing is that whoever lives here afterwards, whether it is one of our children or not, that they enjoy it."

ABOVE: A delicate tracery of hornbeam will thicken during the year to form a protective screen surrounding the lawn: a still centre to the garden; devoid of busy planting, filled with space for contemplation.

OPPOSITE: In front of a tin workshop is the picturesque vegetable garden. Mixed, brightly coloured tulips edge the four raised beds before the crops emerge. A lovely idea; they are left in after flowering.

175

ANDY **STURGEON**

I waited several months before I was able to see Andy Sturgeon's garden. The weather, his dog, his other commitments and his three boys combined to make it imperfect for some of the year and yet this is also part of the garden's charm. This is clearly a family garden rather than one for show.

My expectations were whetted after first seeing the tiny garden Andy has designed for himself and colleagues behind his studio in Brighton. Here he has managed to create a wonderful oasis in a minute space, using many of the techniques deployed in his home garden: a limited colour palette, large tree ferns and dramatic lighting. It is a microcosm of his home garden, which is, in fact, across the road.

Entering the 1870s terraced house, where Andy has lived since 2001, I found Cameron (nine) cooking pasta in a rather chaotic kitchen. Sturgeon juggles single parenthood (his partner, Sarah, died in 2010); a landscape design practice with commissions worldwide; writing books and articles for newspapers; and presenting for television. But despite these undertakings, he has also won five gold medals at Chelsea and is one of the UK's

PREVIOUS SPREAD: The boardwalk snakes, s-shaped through the glade of trees from different continents, embracing a secluded resting place. Cushions by Paola Lenti mirror the curves.

ABOVE: Proof that even the smallest plot can make a great garden. Lighting (from the white bulbous tube on the left), furniture (including a pot with an added glass table top from IKEA), plants and limestone were taken from three different Chelsea gardens to make this area of relaxation at Sturgeon's studio.

OPPOSITE: Rusted steel owls hold tea lights, adding atmosphere in front of the large, glossy-leafed *Viburnum rhytidophyllum*, with yew beneath and bamboo on the right: a bewitching woodland.

leading garden designers. His modern designs fuse strong, contemporary styling with natural materials and innovative planting. He is celebrated for creating bold, architectural and timeless landscapes.

Sturgeon (once dubbed the Michael Caine of gardening), is strong-featured and dynamic but also whimsical. His gardens, and his personal plot in particular, are not dissimilar. His own garden is powerfully structured and dramatically textured, yet has the

There is a fabulous contrast between the *Pseudopanax crassifolius* (lancewood), an evergreen tree from New Zealand with dark, spiny, pointing leaves about one metre long, and the soft, pale fronds of *Dicksonia antarctica*.

OPPOSITE: Looking back, the house is hidden in a world of green.

In front of the raised ground-floor kitchen is a decked balcony with steel railing and wooden steps down to the entrance of the garden, where phlomis and *Hakonechloa macra* grow on one side of a gravel path with a yew cube on the other. This part is, as Andy points out, "arranged like a picture, or a shop window, to be looked at." A living arch conceals what lies beyond, adding mystery and surprise as one anticipates the next part of the garden, which needs to be experienced by being in it.

A serpentine, steel-edged boardwalk leads through ferns (*Polystichum setiferum and P. polyblepharum*), grasses and Solomon's seal. On either side and above is a tunnel of bamboo, dense arching shrubs, and silver birch, ending in a clearing. Here tree ferns slant upwards, framing views and providing a luxurious canopy, whilst below, two round cushions (from Chelsea 2008) covered in yachting rope (so they are mould resistant and suitable for outdoors) sit on top of a curvaceous area of small, black, granite setts. Further on is a lawn edged by a stainless-steel rill (in which the children used to sail small boats) with box, *Olearia macrodonata*, pittosporum, euphorbia, nandina and acanthus on either side. At the end of the garden is a shed, compost heap and some climbing frames which, now that the children are older, Andy will remove, gaining a new space, which, he says, "will be quite liberating. I will have a seating area at the end, made from 2012 Chelsea's paving."

Andy's boys now use the garden less and the lawn has become too small for football, however, he says that his dog never stops using, and destroying, the garden. The space is also used for entertaining and, as with most of Andy's gardens, he uses lighting to great effect. Here the lights enable him to eat outside in the evening and, he explains, give him an enjoyable journey when taking kitchen refuse down to the compost heap, plus they provide a glimpse of the garden at night from inside. For, to Andy, perhaps the most important thing about the garden is to be able to look out of windows and see greenery. When he moved in, the house was isolated from the garden, but by creating steps from the basement and from the raised ground floor, he has made a strong connection, and the garden now flows out from the anchored house. Andy also admits to using the garden for therapy: for example, winding down after flower shows and broadcasting by gardening and getting his hands dirty is very important to him. "I spent most of this morning trying to get the dirt out of my nails", he comments endearingly.

There are many aspects of this garden that work brilliantly. First, the planting is surprising and clever, in spite of the fact that the garden is north facing with dry, chalky soil and, according to Andy, "a massive snail problem so that things that thrive are quite limited".

enchanting atmosphere of a forest glade. It is 45 metres long and 5 metres wide. Being a long, thin, English town garden, comparisons between this and Pearson's plot in Peckham arise. Both, remarkably, are divided into five segments – partitioning is a really useful way of dealing with this shape – but in other respects they are very different. Pearson's is softer and more colourful, whereas Sturgeon's is a much greener, enveloping space that relies on a more restricted plant list and more structure. Yet both, whilst using different means, achieve a sense of other-worldliness and escapism.

Andy bought his house because of the size of the garden: in the heart of Brighton most gardens are tiny. At that time there was grass, a pear tree and a birch, crazy paving, a few sheds, lots of bindweed and a pond. Andy had a plan, which he drew up, though he did the work in stages. He wanted to hide boundaries, so he planted shrubs and climbers, and to create the feeling of a visual and physical journey, which is why he divided the garden into different areas.

The overall impression is almost of an English woodland, but the addition of three large tree ferns and just a few sub-tropical plants gives great impact and strong presence, which, rather than feeling incongruous, add another dimension. The marrying of British plants with those from abroad creates an exotic atmosphere that feels like somewhere else, though nowhere specific.

Texture and movement are also skillfully achieved. Thin, straight, black bamboo sways above the light-green, lacy leaves of lady ferns and the fine, deep-green, grass-like clumps of *Luzula nivea*. *Astelia nervosa*, with its sword-shaped, woolly-topped leaves, thrives under a silver birch. Yet Andy claims to have grown several plants for their historical or ethno-botanical interest, rather than their appearance, and to have chosen robust plants that withstand damage from the children and dog. Tough plants and materials can also be useful in clients' gardens, he says, where longevity is important so that the vision does not disappear after Andy has left.

When asked what advice he would give to someone without a garden designer, Sturgeon replied: "Don't use too many different plants, even in a big garden. It is a mistake very often made – I made it for years – but it is all about what you leave out with plants, materials and objects. Also, you should always remember that you are creating a *place*; somewhere that has atmosphere and hopefully, some heart and soul. That's more important than exactly what it looks like and where you put the furniture."

Andy's garden is peaceful as well as exciting: the tunnel at the start creates a feeling of escapism – entering another world. As he explains, "It is something that I do quite a lot; going from one space to another by going through some sort of doorway." This is also a device used since the Arts and Crafts movement, to create different garden rooms. Andy continues, "You know as you get older, you go to get something from a room and when you get there you can't remember why you went – well, apparently, something happens psychologically when you walk through a doorway, triggering your brain. And something I like about garden design generally is tapping into deep-rooted things in your psyche. Another basic example is that people tend to sit against something where they feel protected and won't get attacked by other people or animals. It is the same in the garden. It is safe and it is green, which is calming."

Andy has managed to completely conceal the fact that this is a very long garden. It is divided into manageable segments providing different experiences. Also clever is the S-shaped, wooden walkway, which hugs the boundary walls on the apex of the curves. This not only gives the illusion that the whole garden is curved rather than straight, but it also makes it feel immensely wider, especially as you emerge from the woodland into the light, airy, sunken patio, where Andy has placed the cushion seats. It demonstrates that the potential for a long, narrow garden, if inventively handled, is boundless. Andy even considered children biking or roller-skating down the boardwalk when he made the sitting area. It is a step down so that children cannot crash into seated adults.

There is a strong backbone to this garden with the snaking path, and cubes of yew echoed by ones of wood, all typical of Sturgeon gardens. But this garden is different. Apart from the slightly unkempt children's area, Andy is also less fussy elsewhere. "These boundaries are completely higgledy-piggledy and ramshackle, with falling down walls. If this were a client's garden, I would make them much smarter. But here, at the end of the garden, I am actually going to make the fallen wall more of a feature. Also, I have never really got on top of the bindweed at the back of the garden, but I have never actually minded it. I only sometimes worry when I look up really high and see some bindweed flowers in the top of a tree: then I think, maybe I should do something about that!"

If this were a commissioned garden, Andy says he would probably give the lawn higher priority, which is very often a request. He would also not normally use tree ferns for a client. The ones here, *Dicksonia antarctica*, come from one of his Chelsea gardens. Andy explains: "Like palm trees, they immediately create an atmosphere. They are not quite as full as they could be because of a couple of years of neglect and my dog ripping out the irrigation. But it is the atmosphere that they create that I like. I suppose it is partly a desire to feel that you are transported somewhere else." But tree ferns are high maintenance. "I like gardens to have a sort of permanence. Tree ferns have to be watered in a certain way or they don't thrive, and if you are relying on a client or their gardener, there is an element of jeopardy. Dicksonia are expensive, so you do not want them to die in a few years. When I work in the Mediterranean, I can use different plants – it is about choosing the right plants for the right climate and the right garden."

It is important that tree ferns never dry out, including the trunk. Many people in mainland Britain also give their dicksonia some protection over winter, though Andy does not. He is prepared to take a certain amount of risk in his own garden, where he does all the maintenance himself. Amusingly, he claims, "I tried to get a

gardener but it didn't work out. I couldn't find one that really did what I wanted. I used to be a proper gardener and I found it really frustrating seeing how long it would take someone else to do something that I know I could have done in an hour."

Andy got into gardening through a love of nature and the outdoors. When he was at school, in Surrey, he did lots of adventure training, camping, hill-climbing and walking all over the country, observing nature. He also loved Claremont Gardens (the English landscape gardens in Esher, Surrey) which, when he was a child, had not been restored and were quite wild and very green. He still remembers playing there, inside old rhododendrons, looking up at the shapes of trunks and the colour of the bark.

However, Andy nearly joined the army, which he maintains, "In a bizarre way was for the same reason as I became a gardener: being outside a lot and being in touch with nature." But instead of the forces, Andy worked with his elder brother, Neil, a landscape constructor. "I started out mixing concrete and the plants came a bit later." He trained at the Welsh College of Horticulture, studied tropical plants, worked at RHS Wisley, then for a garden designer and later set up a garden maintenance business, before becoming a garden designer himself and setting up his own practice. Now, his ingenious designs are often inspired by modern architecture, paintings, bars, film sets or shop windows. He also aims to reflect his clients' personality – noticing, for example, how they dress and the car they drive.

Sturgeon (like Stuart-Smith), has been quoted as saying that he is a Modernist but not a minimalist. He explains that he thinks that currently there is a new English style of garden that various designers achieve in different ways. For example, Tom Stuart-Smith has embraced the prairie-style of planting, but Andy believes that while this extends the season into winter, it only works on a large scale and is also high maintenance. Andy, unusually, is a fan of shrubs, which, he claims are more enduring. But, as he says, "We are all rooted in tradition in some way, but are also contemporary. I change my style to suit the project – it might be a garden for a new-build house, or a period one – and each is different. But the key elements of all my gardens are that they are quite architectural and sculptural: whether that is walls, or blocks of yew, or an actual sculpture that I have designed." Andy enjoys a holistic approach to garden design, sometimes, for instance, designing the furniture too.

OPPOSITE: Green tones and textures tingle: yew, aquilegia, alchemilla, a fading forget-me-not, *Symphytum officinalis* (with white flower), the palmate, bronze-tinged leaves of *Rodgersia podophylla* and the spiky hummock of vivid green *Hakonechloa macra*.

One example of this was his gold medal-winning garden for Chelsea Flower Show 2012, which celebrated the Arts and Crafts movement. Sturgeon used natural materials, country garden planting, an asymmetric quality, and striking walls, which divided the plot in the way that hedges do in Hidcote Manor, for example. He designed a 'floating' oak bench as well as the focal point, a dramatic 'energy wave' sculpture, crafted in copper rings that wove through the garden, spilling across borders and emerging in a rectangular pool. The copper circles were echoed in the walls and in the planting, which included several umbellifers and domed, clipped holly. The whole was a dazzling accomplishment, combining intrigue and exceptional design – like the majority of Sturgeon's gardens. Though he sometimes designs large, classical country, and public gardens, Andy is best known for his contemporary urban gardens (a niche market, he maintains, as most rich people want traditional). One example (very different from

his personal plot) is a private roof terrace, 160 metres square, six storeys up, in the Isle of Dogs in London (see p.186). This fabulous garden succeeds on many levels. It is calming, beguiling and remarkable in that it replicates a river in the air – a strong visual connection with the docks and the river Thames below. Designed for a client in his late twenties, it also includes a gas firepit for entertaining, a hot tub and a putting green.

Opposite. Andy being interviewed for television in his garden for Chelsea 2012. He is very proud of the cantilevered bench he designed, believing strongly that it is part of the garden, working with everything else.

Copper rings and round holes cut into the Jurassic Malt limestone are like chocolate bubbles floating through the garden. Planting softens hard edges in hues of green, white, pink and blue. Here polystichum (fern), aquilegia, *Cenolophium denudatum* (similar to cow parsley) and Paeonia 'Claire de Lune.'

Andy is equally adept at designing for more classical architecture, as the garden for a Georgian house in Chelsea proves. His interesting brief was that the garden should be like a Vermeer painting. The York stone paving has a link with the tiles often depicted in the paintings, while the Portland stone wall bounces light into the garden. The planting uses a lot of green but also warm browns, mustards and pastel blues. The undulating curve (as in his own garden) also adds an illusion of width. Where Andy has triumphed is in avoiding the more obvious route of symmetry and formality so often deployed with period properties.

Sturgen's own garden is even less constrained than his commissioned gardens and it is largely composed of infinite shapes and shades of green. At the time of my visit, some verdant, tiered, candelabra-like phlomis were in bud. Andy intriguingly reveals: "I hate the yellow flower, but it looks so good when it is in leaf, and then in bud, and then when the flowers are finished, that I can put up with the yellow for that short period. Most people like colour and flowers, but green

Below: Timber decking reminiscent of jetties, a beach of river-washed pebbles, a shallow pool reflecting the sky and wooden cubes like tower blocks, all synthesise with the location in the Isle of Dogs, London.

OPPOSITE: A common feature of Sturgeon's work is sensuous curves. Here, the serpentine bench in a client's garden in Chelsea is both sculptural and an ingenious solution to entertaining in a small space: it accommodates countless guests without the spatial limitations of freestanding furniture.

creates a sense of peacefulness, which can be maintained for months on end. You can go into the garden and you are immediately being massaged by the greenery."

Andy's plot reminds me of the lines from *The Garden* by Andrew Marvell (1621–1678):

> Meanwhile the mind from pleasures less,
> Withdraws into its happiness...
> Annihilating all that's made
> To a green thought in a green shade.

MADE **WIJAYA**

Bali conjures images of beaches, Gauguin-like landscapes, gods, spirits, and tropical exoticism. On arrival one is greeted with smiles, brilliant sarongs, pungent cloves and a cacophony of cicadas and frogs. Staying, one sees ceremonies performed, terraces holding emerald rice, and houses and shrines crowded together behind stone walls. Cock fighting, cremations, and Kecak (ritual dancing) are all public spectacles. Bali is theatrical; so is Made Wijaya and so is his garden.

'Made Wijaya' could, in fact, be said to be a stage name. Born Michael White in Sydney, Australia, he actually comes from a long line of Lancastrian clog dancers. His grandfather and two brothers used to dance with Charlie Chaplin and Stan Laurel. Charlie and Stan went to America and the three White brothers went to Sydney. So Made's background is from the stage and he admits that 'theatrical nature' is his middle name. He is flamboyant, outspoken, eloquent and witty. He is also

knowledgeable about all things tropical, and speaks the three Balinese languages fluently. Humility, on the other hand – deriving from the Latin *humus*, meaning earth or ground – a quality found in many gardeners, is not foremost amongst Made's virtues.

Michael White arrived in Bali in 1973. The story goes that he jumped ship and swam ashore in a rainstorm. He had been a student of architecture and wanted a short break, but he fell under the spell of the Balinese people and their culture and stayed. He had a variety of different jobs, including teaching English and tennis ("I was a sort of child tennis star"), although he claims that actually, all his life he wanted to be a ballet dancer. He also fell into a job as a photojournalist with *The Bali Post*. Then an old friend from Australia, "from the cocktail party circuit", pronounced, "You've done architecture, you can design a garden for me." Made's mother had been a good gardener but he had never really done much himself. This garden happened to be for a house designed by Geoffrey Bawa, a very influential Sri Lankan architect and the principal force behind what is known globally as 'tropical modernism'. So Made started with a good client and a great piece of architecture.

Remarkably, it was not long before Made was asked to design the garden for the legendary Bali Oberoi Hotel, and he has never looked back. Made travelled widely in Asia, carried out research, and is now a recognised authority on tropical garden design and architecture. He is Southeast Asia's most renowned landscape architect, and has designed over 600 gardens in Bali, Singapore, India, Mexico, Hawaii, America and Morocco. They include the Bali Hyatt and Amandari Resorts, and David Bowie's former Mustique estate. Wijaya also lectures at the National University of Singapore, has written eight books, has a signature website 'Stranger in Paradise – Diary of an expatriate in Bali' and a blog.

His garden, home and company, P.T. Wijaya Tibwana International (which employs over 100 people), are based at Villa Bebek, on the fringes of Sanur, on the southern coast of Bali. The walled exterior, with five gates, is a bit like a Balinese village streetscape. It is a good neighbourhood but it is still quite rural, with the sound of distant waves, fishermen nearby and Javanese soup vendors congregating outside. Entering the compound one is immediately beguiled by the traditional design, where the interplay of courtyards and architecture is integral. Here in the Tropics, warmth and fertility are constant, and the distinction between indoors and out evaporates.

Traditional Balinese village homes consist of several largely open structures made of wood, with high-pitched roofs (usually thatched). These buildings are often referred to as pavilions, and

are grouped round a courtyard bordered by a high wall. There are separate structures for the kitchen, sleeping areas, bathing and shrine. An extended family of around fifteen, plus a few dogs and a pig might live here. Sometimes six or more families share a compound where, in addition to the other pavilions, there might be a granary or rice barn, funeral parlour, dance theatre and an ancestral temple.

The orientation of the buildings, as well as the worship of good spirits, and the placation or avoidance of evil ones, is essential. Flowers, coconut leaves and fruit are needed as offerings, so the courtyards often incorporate some tropical trees (such as palms, banana, guava and rambutan) and flowering shrubs. Flowers are also put behind the ears after prayers. The frangipani tree is found in almost all Balinese temple gardens (and there are more temples than homes in Bali), as the scented flowers are the gods' favourite. Frangipanis, with their upstretched branches, are also a signature plant of Made Wijaya.

Villa Bebek was built in 1990 as the Bali residence of a former Miss Palm Beach (Sydney). It was Made's biggest private house commission as architect and designer. In 1997 Made bought the property, which consisted of a house, a cottage and two rental villas. He knocked down some of the interlocking walls, giving a 'ruinscape' feeling and added many gates to what is basically now one large compound, which increased organically, as did the redesigned gardens. Made wanted everyone, including guests and employees, to look at a beautiful garden. His work incorporates four divisions: Wijaya Words (his publications), landscape, interior design and architecture. He describes his plot as, "living over the shop, but horizontally".

The layout of the whole compound and the style of the gardens are classically Balinese. There are 10 buildings and over 60 intimate courtyards, peopled with statues and shrines, and linked by a maze of paths, ponds, paving, pergolas and of course, plants. It is the landscaping that binds all the activities of the Villa Bebek into a harmonious whole. It is poetic and romantic but is also very sculpted. Five full-time gardeners have maintained the garden for 25 years. It is around 0.3 hectares, but a lot of that is buildings, walls and gates – all adding privacy – that nevertheless are very much a part of the whole. Each

pavilion opens onto garden terraces on at least two sides. Rooms are stacked with antiques and drawing boards: as Made playfully puts it, "The houses' interiors are annuals, not perennials – major changes are wrought overnight to accommodate the expectations of guests or to provide a new studio for a project."

Both inside and out are works in progress, like an art factory undergoing constant change. Gates are repainted, sample statues, signage or lamps are added to walls, and might later be used on another project. Made can test how these look and weather in his own garden before suggesting them to clients. Change, as well as activity, is constant. There are 90 people for lunch every day at Villa Bebek, including master gardeners and artisans. So whilst it is possible to find a secluded spot in the garden, one will also see a woman in formal Balinese dress float

ABOVE: A composition in grey. Here a Jepun pedestal fountain designed by Wijaya is set beside the branches of a miniature frangipani, in front of a grey stone wall holding a carved Balinese soapstone panel. Made maintains that the correct placement of art in the garden is crucial.

OPPOSITE: Various guardian statues huddle (not unlike gnomes) under a *Pisonia alba* in this central court, in front of the design studio. They are placed on a *compang*, or raised stone platform. Typically here, it is surrounded by a collection of ancient art as well as a modern Australian landscape painting on the ochre wall, for Made enjoys the primitive-modern mix.

through with offerings to place on a shrine, gardeners, household staff, draftsmen and secretaries bustling about their business, and Made, multitasking, giving constant instruction. Real Balinese gardens, Made explains, including his own, but unlike those in shopping malls, combine mystery derived from ornamental statues and the spirits that inhabit the shrines;

romance, because the Balinese love nature; practicality and vitality. As he talks, two doves are drinking from the prototype fountain he designed, as if to endorse his words. "I find a lot of today's New Asian or Zen-style gardens have a treeless, loveless, lifeless, godless look. The gates on a Balinese house are always open. Stray dogs come in, knowing where they can drink from a pond. There are always animals crossing, and people traversing, with trayloads of offerings to give the statues that are empowered. There are about fifteen shrines in my garden, which are all active. In Bali every house is a bit like a Japanese monastery."

Made's commissioned gardens tend to be static. They are designed and then maintained, whereas Villa Bebek is always evolving. The planting schemes are also eclectic, irreverent and whimsical, but with classic bones, because it is a rectilinear series of courtyards. The theme tree of the garden is the

frangipani (plumeria), and when you are in one of the three buildings with a second floor, the flowers are right by your face. Wijaya also brings some more unusual plants to his garden, such as crinums, with their long strap-shaped leaves and umbels of stunning, narrow-tepalled, funnel-like, fragrant, white flowers. He likes scented shrubs such as ixoras, with their red, orange and pink, hyacinth-like blooms, as well as shrubs that flower in the wet season, such as the Peacock Bush (caesalpinia). However, this is not essentially a plantsman's garden and Made does not talk a great deal about his plants. He likes to think about his garden as a "museum of living art: a rambling, surrealist source of inspiration".

Walking around Villa Bebek, one can only marvel at the network of ornate, interlocking courtyards, which in progression seem endlessly varied and exotic. Each is like a different stage set including scenery, props and set design. It is common for garden writers to use terminology of the theatre, such as 'centre stage', 'spotlight position' and 'backdrop', but at Villa Bebek it is especially appropriate.

There is attention to detail everywhere, for example in the paving, such as the small squares of stone (in the Japanese tradition) with what Made terms 'grass grouting'. This works on several levels, aesthetic and textural. He does a similar thing with larger stepping-stones made from the limestone he brought out of West Java and used at the Bali Hyatt and the Amandari. Now, he says, this is copied everywhere, not always tastefully. At Villa Bebek, care is also given to the placing of the myriad artefacts and works of art, all of which are both softened and enlivened by the planting. The compound is full and intense, mirroring the bright light and extreme heat, as well as the jungle nearby.

Each courtyard holds a vista as well as a lure to explore further. Views are repeatedly framed so that one stops to gaze, while verandahs provide inviting shade, seating and solace. Ponds are filled with tropical plants, statues and fountains, and form natural up-lighting. Water cools and splashes, stone monkeys grimace, carved wooden doorways and gates intrigue, trees twist, and palm fronds and ferns stripe the ground with brightness and shadow. The turquoise swimming pool triggers further amazement. One immediately recalls Hockney's Californian pool paintings in its wiggly lap lines. Beside it, are a picturesque pergola, a folly-like water tower, inspired by old Moorish palaces, and three decorative gates.

The aim in creating a Balinese garden such as Made's is to find a balance between the natural and man-made, the ornamental and the mystical, resulting in a sense of well-being and tranquillity. This could be compared with Japan where, as in Bali, the garden is designed to be viewed from a terraced pavilion. Like Arab, Persian and Indian gardens, Balinese ones are both outdoor living spaces and places of beauty. The courtyard floor is typically swept earth or red brick. Delicate vines drape from pillars, and orchids and birdcages are hung from trees. The garden is also fecund, dripping with ferns and moss, but like kinetic art, it requires control. The growing cycle is exaggerated in the Tropics so a secret to success is the air and light.

Made does not do much gardening himself now as he has a bad knee, but because he was good at tennis, he had a strong

Swimming pools in the Tropics are symbols of escape and comfort. This one is stunning with its Hockneyesque wavy lines. Beside it is the breakfast terrace, shaded by fishtail palms.

forearm and used to be good with a machete. He recalls, "I was far the best hacker, and the English tourists at the Oberoi would all shriek, because in England you get out tiny clippers and take a few leaves off, whereas here you really have to cut things off at the ankles once a year, before the wet season." Made used to stay on and maintain the gardens he designed for large hotels, because he loved it, but regrets that eventually a general manager would come along and want to see the whole view and chop all the trees down while Made was away. This is obviously not a problem at Villa Bebek, where he is in control of his empire. As he puts it, very descriptively, "If it is your own garden, you are basting it every day. It is encrusted and personal and on the edge of fecundity. You cannot gift someone else a garden that needs that level of maintenance."

Made's own garden is considerably more lush and full than if he had designed it for a client. Here flowers and plants are allowed to flourish wildly, giving a comfortable, un-manicured feel. As he concedes, "This is sometimes a problem for people who come to see me in my office and expect a fashionable, resort-type garden with timber-slatted screens and scatter Buddhas. You couldn't do this for a client. My whole life is in it. This garden *is* my life." It is full of personal touches, like a brick with 'India' written on it that he got from a visit there. The garden also mirrors his irreverent sense of humour, playfully mixing art and religion in the form of demons and guardian figures. Occasionally, Made will deliberately add a bit of kitsch or exceptionally bright colour.

In Villa Bebek, each courtyard is carefully composed and has a theme, often reliant on colour. Two are white sand courts, a look originating from old Sanur coastal gardens which has

nearly disappeared now. In one, the ground is white sand crossed by square limestone stepping-stones. The walls are white and the courtyard is largely planted with white cacti. A pedestal pot of *Aloe vera* is a striking accent with a lantern beneath. Ground cover is provided by tradescantia and hemigraphis, while an antique, carved stone panel from a Balinese mountain village is set into the wall for added interest. This court is viewed from three rooms and also acts as a private yard for a bedroom. But as Made delightfully expresses

OPPOSITE: The staff terrace, next to the entrance, has a backdrop of brilliant blue, as the compound walls are here painted with a powdered pigment from Morocco. Paving stones with 'grass grouting' are a feature that unifies different areas of the whole.

ABOVE: The garden for this private client's villa in Bali shows an expansive style. Through the leaves of a frangipani tree, lie a curved infinity pool with echoing grass terrace, merging with the sea beyond.

statues, which always have blue in them. As he puts it, "Unlike a lot of landscapers today, who like chrome and glass in the garden, I am a colourist."

His earlier, more famous gardens for hotels and resorts are what he describes as 'English tropical artful natural'. His work is classical and traditional, with the exception, perhaps, of the Tirtha Resort, but he considers himself a Modernist, because that does not necessarily mean a minimalist. Some of his gardens, such as the Villa Kirana near Ubud, are expansive, merging with the country beyond, with its views of the Ayung river gorge and verdant rice terraces. Some others have open views of the sea. However, Made believes that his real skill, "and no one really competes with me commercially, or professionally, is in doing microcosms or courtyards."

Made has the passion of the convert. He felt it was his mission when he came to Indonesia to put down all the herbaceous borders of the

it, courtyard gardens are a reversal of the norm: "Guests enjoy vistas into the interiors from the garden". Often the interior design becomes the backdrop for the landscaped space, while vice versa, each window also frames an elegant view.

Made continues, "As I look out of my number one man's window, which is in front of mine, I look onto a primitive courtyard with stone dolmen [table] from East Indonesia, where the predominant colour is ochre, and I found a lovely, primitive, naïve bed that I put onto the verandah so it is a sleeping platform for the staff. I love hybridisation." He has also always loved the lapis lazuli blue which Jacques Majorelle (the French painter who created the Majorelle Garden in 1924) used in Marrakech. Made uses it as a background for his classic Balinese

Dutch colonial era. The style was very municipal so, with his research and his love of the architecture, he developed his own style. His Lea Asian Garden in the Naples Botanical Garden in Florida, USA, is one of his latest passions, and he considers it, in a way, to be an extension of the Villa Bebek. He told me, "It is still a very young garden, but I think that one day it will be called a masterpiece because it is so rare. There is a category in jewellery, where people do rare and exquisite work and they are not considered to be arrogant, they are just saying what they are. I think I am versatile, though some people say all my gardens look the same. I feel that you can detect my signature because my gardens are poetic, romantic and they are exuberant." The Villa Bebek acts as muse for Made's commissioned work and combines these three qualities in extreme.

JACQUES **WIRTZ**

Jacques Wirtz was born in Schoten, a suburb of Antwerp, in 1924. After studying landscape architecture, he started his own business in 1950. His sons Martin and Peter joined the firm in 1990. The design studio Wirtz International, with its sister construction firm Wirtz Tuinarchitectuur, is the largest landscape design business in Belgium, with private, public, corporate and institutional clients. When Jacques received the Golden Medal of the Royal Flemish Academy of Belgium for Science and the Arts in 2006, he was compared with André Le Nôtre, William Kent and Lancelot 'Capability' Brown. He is renowned for his harmonious designs that work with the spirit of the place and with its architecture. He is revered for an ability to provide experiences both of invigoration and peace in his gardens. In addition, he is acclaimed for his virtuoso trademark – the revolutionary use of sculpted hedges – and his painterly approach to herbaceous planting.

These qualities are also found in Jacques' home garden, though in this case there was never any preconceived plan. The Wirtz family (there are four children) moved into a modest house, formerly a gardener's cottage, in Botermelkdijk, near Schoten, in 1970. Jacques and his wife, Wilhelmina, still live here. They had lived only a few minutes down the road before, and Jacques knew the property when he was a child, secretly playing in the woods. It was a perfect plot as he was in dire need of more space for the business. The office and nursery (for it is a design/build company) is where a farm and pastureland used to be (a brick barn still bears bullet holes from the war). The house is separated from the office by a beech wood and an eighteenth-century moat; it is now screened by beech hedges along the perimeters, and hornbeam beside the house, both planted by Jacques to give privacy.

Because Jacques is in his late eighties, although I met him, and he told me that to his mind "Sissinghurst is the Vatican of gardens", it was his son Peter, described by Jacques as "my spiritual successor", who showed me round the garden. Both are tall and gracious and share the same smile. They both clearly adore the place. The house is attractive, so the garden enters into a dialogue with it, rather than attempting to overwhelm it. The back windows all look onto the garden. Closest to the house is a box enclosure of yew topiaries of different shapes, and the reflections of green enter the house, throwing their incandescence onto the white walls. When Peter was a child, the first thing he saw every morning from his bedroom window was the garden. Now this room is the place where his mother irons.

When the Wirtzes moved in, the 2.5-hectare garden had been untouched since the war and was covered in brambles and nettles that were 2 metres high. It was formerly the vegetable garden and orchard of a great estate, and the soil is very fertile, sandy loam.

The structure, divided into four by a cruciform path, flanked with box hedges, existed and has been kept. Around the front and back of the ivy-clad house is clipped box too, of different cultivars, providing decorative intimacy. The entrance is, in fact, similar to a typical pastor's house in Flanders. Peter gave me this fascinating explanation: Belgium, being a Catholic country, celebrates Palm Sunday, and in Flemish, the word for palm is the popular word for boxwood (since there is no word for palms that are native to

Jerusalem). So on Palm Sunday the members of the congregation
bring a freshly cut branch of boxwood to church and afterwards,
they either put it behind a little crucifix in their house, or plant it.
That is why box is so prevalent in this area; it is also the plant with
which Jacques Wirtz is most strongly identified.

Wirtz demonstrated that a hedge, this simplest of elements,
could become the star attraction in a garden. He uses hedges

PREVIOUS SPREAD: The entrance to the front of the house is typical Wirtz: a
hedge of mixed cultivar box, clipped balls and squares of box, castellated
hornbeam; all in different shades of green, forming layers of pruned texture,
merging with the backdrop of the mature oak, ash and sycamore boundary.

ABOVE: At the back of Jacques' house, curvaceous yew topiary is bound by
box. A screen of beech adds spatial organisation, while apple leaves and
frost, like flaked almonds and suger, dust 'buns' of box.

in a Modernist way, instead of metal and glass, liberating them from formal convention to create spaces of originality and mystique. But in his own garden this occurred almost by accident. Along both sides of the cruciform paths, but particularly along the immense length of the main axis of the garden, as far as the eye can see, is a justly iconic, astounding avenue of cloud-pruned boxwood. Individual box mounds huddle together and mesh into a cushioning, amorphous, billowing whole. When Jacques moved in, these box trees, after 30 years of neglect, had grown wild, lanky and gappy. Knowing they formed the backbone of the garden, Jacques fed and clipped them, but in an inspired moment he decided to go against rectilinear tradition that was probably their original incarnation, and go for a practical solution.

As Peter puts it, "Every year the sparse branches became these organic forms. There was no big theory; the shears followed the natural shapes. Each year in the snow, they fall apart a little bit and so it changes all the time. When we occasionally have French visitors, they do not understand that there is no philosophy behind it, but there is none. Nature suggested it. Because my father went to Japan a lot in the late '60s and '70s, it has been said that this hedge has Japanese influence, but it does not. I will tell you no lies."

On the right, the garden is bordered by a wall, beside which is a greenhouse and a raised reflective pond, all three also already in situ. In fact, rather than design this garden, Peter says, "We filled it in". Further back is a holding area for the business – a bit like an artist's studio where paintings are stashed against walls. Here, topiarised trees of holly, yew and various kinds of box in different shapes nestle and vie for attention. Some large boxwood specimens here were offered to Jacques by farmers

in the early 1970s, when box was unpopular and difficult to sell. As Peter declares with understatement, "My father made them more popular in my country". Peter and his brother, Martin, share a fascination with box, which Peter started to trial as a child. He still has a specimen that was given to him in the form of a small cutting as a present from an Italian nursery. It now lives amongst the trees for future use in clients' gardens, but it is not for sale.

Since Peter was about ten, he and his family all worked in the garden, weeding, clipping and mowing. Each child had their own part, and Peter recalls that his father "was very strict", although Peter also describes the garden as "a paradise for a child". Peter started by growing radishes, courgettes and tomatoes (which filled the windowsill of his bedroom). "There were hundreds of tomatoes", Peter remembers with relish. "My mother cooked

very well, so we learned to appreciate food very young. She made a wonderful dish called Courgettes Provençal. It is made with green courgettes and red tomatoes, and I said, 'I will grow everything in yellow', and I succeeded, with Suttons Seeds, but it didn't taste very good!" However, like all children, the Wirtzes played as well as gardened. "We had some pleasure areas, such as a box parterre filled with roses. The box was in place when my father bought the house, but we children rode our bicycles through it so it became transparent and not like it is now."

OPPOSITE: The living sculpture that is Jacques' cloud-pruned hedge, with its seemingly limitless abstract undulations, takes your breath away.

BELOW: This filigree of winter branches is enlivened by the apparent movement in the hedge, which has taken on a life of its own.

ABOVE: Waves of colour in Jacques' garden mark the changing seasons. Here mauve *Kalimeris incisa* 'Blue Star' interspersed with maroon *Knautia macedonica* and tall bronze fennel, combine in a froth, like iridescent bubbles.

OPPOSITE: In winter the structure of the garden comes to the fore. Hard and soft lines, grandeur and intimacy, light, space and form, converge.

Box, yew, hornbeam and beech are signature plants. Hedges are a way of counteracting flatness, defining spatial sequences and views, adding layers, depth and drama throughout the year. They contrast with what Peter terms the weakness of perennial borders. In winter, the garden is almost greener than in the summer, with the powerful presence of the box, as well as the yews and hollies in the nursery beds. Then the beech hedges turn copper, adding interest, for the Wirtz family all clearly delight in colour, as well as fruit and flowers. They retained many of the original apple trees and an ancient mulberry, and have planted more old varieties of apples as well as espaliered pears. Flowers are planted in rows and blocks (reminiscent of a cutting garden, or perhaps Chelsea Physic Garden, which Peter loves) rather than

borders, in what Peter terms, 'My mother's kingdom'. Delphiniums, gaura, nasturtiums, irises, tree peonies and flowering shrubs are grown in trial beds, partly as experiments, to examine their performance for use in commissioned gardens. "We are big rose freaks", admits Peter, claiming that when he looks at David Austin's catalogue he feels drunk! Through a gate to the left, a 'secret' test garden is filled with roses of all varieties.

Jacques was also a pioneer in the use of grasses as vital structure in the garden, for texture is another outstanding attribute of Wirtz gardens. Grasses, mounded lawns and water are used to create sweeping lines in contrast to bold modern offices, or to soften and divide areas of private gardens. In Jacques' own garden, grasses and seedheads sway sensually. Peter also talks of parallels between leaves and "human skin, either soft or of rougher, coarser texture". Here there are prickles, grey hairs, leatheriness and smooth gloss.

All these elements in the Wirtz garden coexist and juxtapose. Topiary shapes, columnar trees and rounded shrubs (that provide

vertical accents, structure and anchorage) combine with perennials and grasses (which add dynamic movement, colour and sprawling seasonality). In this, the garden could be said to have a very twenty-first-century atmosphere, abandoning strict compartmentalism. Other examples are the late Christopher Lloyd's garden at Great Dixter in Sussex; Broughton Grange, designed by Christopher Bradley-Hole; and Piet Oudolf's garden at Hummelo in The Netherlands. It is a design principal which can also be successfully emulated on a smaller scale in many private gardens.

Jacques' own garden is difficult to categorise, and that, in fact, is possibly what makes it so singular. When I talked to Peter about the garden further from the southern side of the house becoming less formal, he gently rebuked me, "We discovered the distinction people make between formality and informality: we never knew there was a distinction and we never make it. To us it is a very artificial and intellectual concept. Nature and landscape architecture do not have these divisions. It is a very limiting debate. Some people say that as soon as you clip a plant, it is formal, but to

me there are so many degrees and subtle variations." The garden is essentially fluid, benefitting from layers of texture, combining many elements, and attaining a perfect balance of wild and tamed, familiar and strange. In a few of Jacques' commissioned projects, such as Cogels Park, in Schoten, this is also true. Amongst ancient woodland and an existing serpentine lake, one comes across oval, pruned trees and mysterious cobblestone pyramids (see p.209).

Peter calls the Wirtz garden "a transformation rather than a design". Jacques recognised the attributes of the existing structure of the site and borrowed them, but it is very rare to have this opportunity when working for a client (although this was the case for Cogels Park). It is also very different from a commissioned garden in that it is two-thirds nursery and one-third private garden. However, the nursery is also beautiful and untypical, and merges with the pleasure garden. Peter used an expression 'private nursery' to describe the whole and in many ways this is very apt. He went on to say, "The nursery is also leisure, because the experimental beds are fun and those parts are always changing."

now gives him sleepless nights. Formed of green rooms made of yew hedges and pleached lime, Peter tells me: "It suffered badly form the heat wave of 2003, when, in a national scandal, hundreds of people died. Hundreds of yews also died, because the irrigation collapsed. The garden is the nail in our coffin, spoilt by vending vans for snacks and because it has become a notorious haunt of prostitutes." As a result, the hedges have had to be cut lower in order to be less concealing. The garden has also, sadly, never been fully completed.

Wirtz's work (for example, the Banque Générale de Luxembourg garden) may sometimes honour the legacy of great eighteenth-century predecessors (such as John Aislabie, who designed Studley Royal in Yorkshire), but it also has its own individual postmodern style. His gardens are characterised by an architectural approach; conscious use of light and shade; a balance of openness and enclosure; a blend of sharp and soft lines; and a combination of tension and quiet. However, the majority of his gardens, whilst containing these stylistic elements, are quite minimal, with relatively few component parts. The Carrousel Garden is a wonderful example of a bold concept: its main feature is a fan pattern of twelve radial yew hedges reminiscent both of amorphous dragons and bullet trains. It is a brilliantly modern take on a traditional European box parterre. His Jubilee Park, in

The Wirtz garden is perfectly maintained by the family as well as two full-time gardeners and one who works part-time. Jacques' wife works in the garden everyday. It looks effortlessly groomed but not manicured. Spray is used minimally on the roses, box and pears. Leaves and apples scatter the ground; seedheads add ethereal winter interest and encourage birds and insects; and the orange, ovate leaves of a hosta dying back echo the beech hedges.

Unfortunately, some of Jacques' other projects do not receive this care, and have not survived in the way that was envisaged. The Carrousel Garden, which connects the Louvre with the Tuileries Gardens in Paris, of which Jacques was most proud,

London's Canary Wharf (designed with Peter) combines undulating lawns, trees (mainly metasequoia), a snaking wall topped with soft grasses, and a serpentine raised canal of flowing water, which twists and turns round jagged corners. Jacques' own garden is much more diverse and 'comfortable', whilst also being both exciting and poetic, arousing a strong emotional response. Whilst containing jaw-dropping features like his cloud hedge, it also holds a free-spirited mix of plants that are trialled for potential clients, along with personal favourites grown purely for pleasure. It expresses the Wirtz personality – as Peter says, "It is our garden. It is us." The garden is not open to the public and retains an intimate and protected atmosphere: that of an extremely special and serene family garden.

This private client's garden in Antwerp is a more minimal version of Wirtz's own, where the eye is drawn through veils of textured planting. Plane trees in the foreground are echoed behind, with fluffy *Pennisetum alopecuroides* backed by higher molinia grasses.

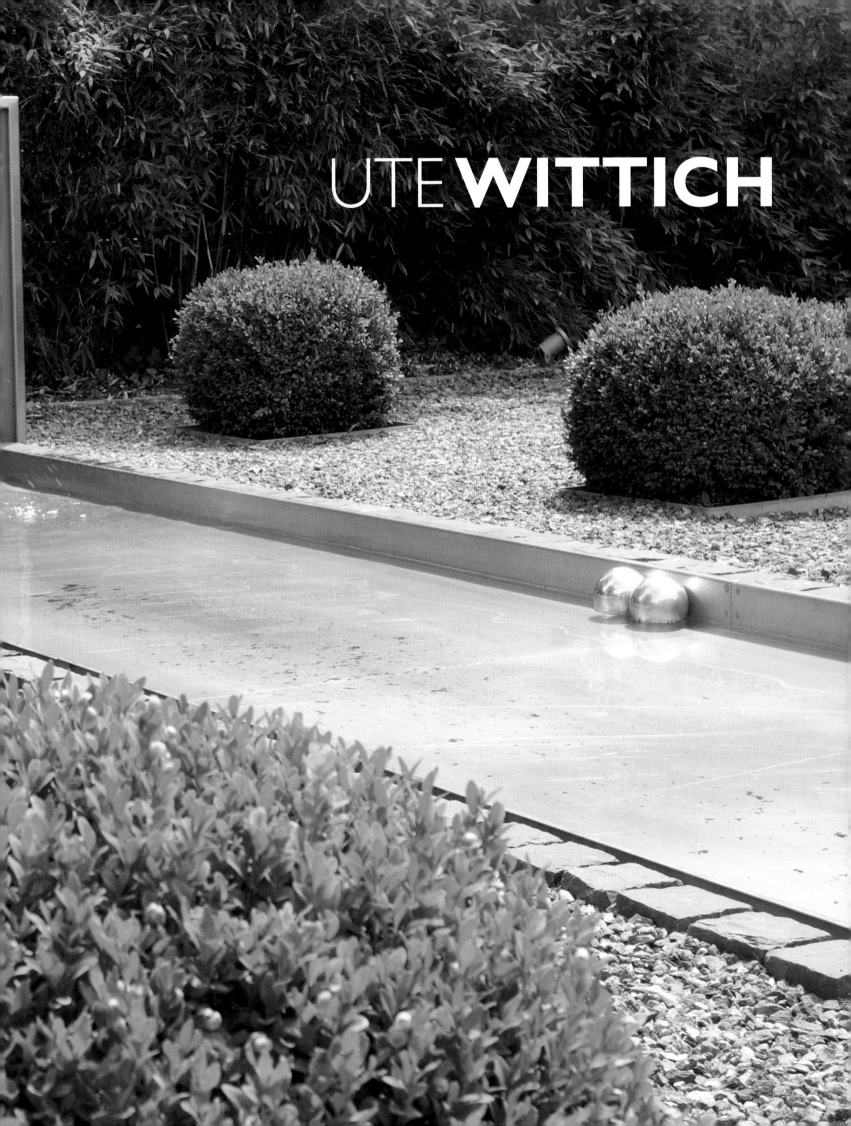

UTE**WITTICH**

PREVIOUS SPREAD: In this client's garden in a Frankfurt suburb, silver balls echo both those of box and the steel edging. A simple, concealed pump enables water to gush from a hole in the wall: a slit in a red mouth. Behind, bamboo provides privacy as well as further movement (see also p.222).

On the wall beside the entrance to Ute's own garden hangs a decorative enamelled thermometer advertising Varta batteries. Its blue background matches the cobalt of the doorframe and even the plastic watering can. It is reminiscent of a café where bright signage creates a jolly scene.

Ute Wittich's house, on the outskirts of Frankfurt, is her home and workplace, and is packed on every floor with figurative African art. Ascending narrow, winding stairs one arrives at her roof garden: a jewel box atop the house. It is tiny, full, bright and beautiful and it makes you smile. Ute herself seems to mirror the garden exactly. She is petite, with a helmet bob of copper-red hair, and clothes and jewellery all in coordinating shades of maroon and orange-red.

The coral-coloured garden walls enclose a decked floor on which stand a long wooden seat and table. All around, on small chairs and tables, windowsills, walls and on the floor are plants in containers, huddling together. The prevailing colours are maroon and pink but there are others too. Ute, who does not normally like yellow flowers, allows a cassia plant here, since it blooms from spring to November, and its long stems connect with the other plants.

There are also myriad greens in leaves. As Ute points out, "There are 30 or 40 different forms, colours and textures of leaves and grasses here. It is important, and if there are enough, you need not have flowers." However, she has not skimped on this front either, with blooms on plants ranging from arum lilies, dicentras, hydrangeas, hostas, tibouchina, violas, roses, clematis, liatris, nepeta, oleander (replaced annually) to apple blossom on a tree. On top of the far wall are red metal planters in the shape of carrier bags, and suspended above these, orange

and pink paper lanterns. The effect is a mix of quirky individuality, with cohesion achieved through attention to placing. There is the air of a Mediterranean café, a holiday refuge, a place to enjoy.

Ute wishes her garden was larger, and says she dreams of a bigger one that would extend straight from the house. But that is not possible here, as the part of the site that might be a garden was, in fact, once a fire station and is her present husband's studio: he is an artist, Bernhard Jäger. They bought the house in 1984 and for them it was perfect, being inexpensive and spacious. Beneath the roof garden is another, this time a courtyard (see p.218). This shady area is also painted coral red but has a stone floor and a large terracotta urn as focal point. It is surrounded by smaller terracotta pots filled with ferns. This is a calm, decorative space, used mainly to walk through, while the garden above is for sitting in. Ute and her husband often eat on the roof terrace and if she is working in her ground-floor studio, Ute will regularly take a break upstairs, to relax in her garden. She finds that moving the pots around and tending the plants is calming and therapeutic.

Bernhard loves the garden too. They go to nurseries together and beforehand he says, "Please don't

LEFT: Containers made of terracotta, plastic and metal, on different levels, hold flowers, grasses, shrubs, trees and climbers, which seem to flow around the walls of the terrace. Personal touches such as a metal ball enliven the space.

OPPOSITE: Everything is placed with loving care for maximum effect, creating an intimate, idiosyncratic and dramatic space.

OPPOSITE: Hard surfaces are softened with ferns and ivy in this still-life arrangement in pink. Quirky detail is added with the painted wooden flowers on the sill.

ABOVE RIGHT: Even this tiny garden is, to an extent, colour co-ordinated. The pink stucco walls, terracotta, arum lilies and gazania (the daisy-like flower in the window box, which closes at night and opens in the sun) all blend in unison.

BELOW RIGHT: Red and orange paper lanterns, red planters and pink hydrangeas are amongst Ute and her husband's favourite colours and, surprisingly, do not clash but glow like jewels in a box.

buy any plants", but once there, he sees plants that he likes and changes his mind, saying, "Let's get that one!" It is something they can enjoy together as well as a place where they can entertain a few friends. Over the front of their house, by the street, grows a vast wisteria. It was growing all over the windows and this year Ute's husband asked her to prune it. She explains graphically, "My heart was bleeding but I did it and it is OK. And now I am thinking of perhaps adding another plant that would be more controllable, like a rose or a vine." She enjoys buying as many plants as possible, rather in the same way as she and Bernhard enjoy collecting African art.

Since all the plants in the garden are in containers, however, they are hard work and have to be watered frequently. Ute tried an automatic watering system but found that it did not work well, so she now does it by hand. Moreover, since many of the plants (such as the cassia) are only half-hardy, they have to be brought indoors during winter. Then Ute's bathrooms become filled with plants. Apparently, Bernhard tries to dissuade incorporating half hardies, but she is a collector, and not easily deterred from this.

Ute has used the carrier-bag planters that are in her garden in commissioned work. The bright colours are somewhat of a trademark, while equisetum (horsetail), grown in her garden, could be said to be a signature plant. But almost all Ute's other designs are contrastingly minimal, relying on straight lines, graphic precision and a more limited colour palette. Her home garden, though only 2 x 4.5 metres, is uniquely personal – a bright nest of hoarded treasures. "The other gardens are very different", Ute says, "I live with this one and can influence it at all times. I love it and so does my husband, but it is just for us. It changes all the time and I do not mind spending a lot of time gardening, but I don't think most clients, ones that do not have a real love of plants, would want to do that. For some clients, a garden is more symbolic, for guests."

Ute tells me that one of her women clients is a really hands-on gardener. She had an olive tree and a fig that suffered during the winter, but the owner talked to the trees and looked after them, and as Ute puts it, "the plants said 'Thank you'". Ute likes dealing

with all sorts of clients so long as they give her some freedom. She tries to explain her ideas and persuade clients to accept them if possible. If, however, they keep arguing against her proposals, she admits that she cannot do the design. Sometimes, Ute says, ideas for a garden come to her straight away, but occasionally, they do not. If the latter happens, she will make an appointment to meet the client, thus imposing a deadline on herself, and the evening before the meeting, the concept will come! Plants are always an important element in her designs. She likes the progression from spring to winter, as well as considering the habitat, the colour of flower and leaf, the texture and the scent.

Ute's appreciation of plants has grown over the years, as has her knowledge of design, since, remarkably, she is untrained. At first a photographer, dabbling in landscape design, she met

an architect, who, surprisingly, offered her a job on a project he was working on. It was an old people's home and he wanted help designing the garden. Through this she met her first husband, an architect with whom she worked, and her experience rocketed. At first she did not know how to give briefs to contractors, but as her work increased so did her

expertise, to the extent that she qualified in 1983, without ever formally studying. Next she started her own landscape architecture practice, always designing both public and private spaces.

Social housing and community projects are of particular

Her first landscape designs tended to be flowing and organic with curved forms. But for the past five or six years, she has developed a more minimalistic style, employing geometric features and straight axes. Ute says, "I love it now", and continues to explain that "it is a bit of a trend now, but what I like is not just only sharp, linear landscaping but the combined contrast of softer planting. I used not to like hedges but their straight, strong forms have become my thing, whether they are buxus, or ones that have autumn colour, like prunus, malus or liquidambar." She admires the work of Jacques Wirtz and Patrick Blanc.

"I like garden rooms, too," Ute says, "so you can take your breakfast in one place, your evening meal in another, while children play in a different area. It also adds a sense of mystery if you do not see the whole garden at once." Ute is also influenced by the new wave of planting and utilises grasses effectively. She likes movement in gardens, and feels that the play of light is important as well. Finally, if Ute is able, she will include water in her designs – whether more natural or formal in style, and whatever the size, for she feels strongly that small gardens can be just as exciting as larger ones.

Ute took me to see two of her designs for clients that certainly bear this out. Both revealed surprises that one would never have expected from the exteriors. The first was a roof terrace, but unlike Ute's, it relied on symmetry and horizontal axes. In a small town outside Frankfurt is a modern housing complex above shops, offices and a gymn. On the third floor there is a stylishly modern apartment with large glass windows leading directly onto the terrace. Nearest the house is an oak-decked seating area ending in a line of still water. Stepping-stones take you to another row of oak decking, beyond which is the garden, also planted in rows. Lines of box, lavender, roses, nepeta, geranium and alliums adorn this dynamic space of soft colours. Sculptural steel pipes from the heating system below rise up in one corner, incorporated into the whole, to animate the scene. All the plants, trees (apple, quince and maple), earth and metal planters had to be craned into the space.

interest to Ute, but she has also designed commercial, historic, public and private spaces in Germany and abroad. She relishes this diversity, expressing it vividly as "the salt in the soup". Ute learned by doing and she found she had a feeling for gardens, enjoying drawing the plans, using plants and colour, the latter, she admits, being very important to her.

Perhaps even more surprising is a small garden behind a house in Eckenheim, a suburb of Frankfurt (see pp.212-3, 222). Behind the house, largely furnished in black and white, is a courtyard-style garden of gravel and stone, with a rill-like, stainless steel, long, rectangular, shallow pond in the middle. On either side is a row of box balls and oblongs next to pivoting metal screens or sails that

turn in the wind. At the back of the pond is a bright red wall, a letter-box-like slit creating a spout through which the water circulates dramatically, hitting metal balls that the owners placed in the pond, making the whole reminiscent of a bowling alley. This garden manages to be serene and electrifying at the same time. Great attention has been paid to details, such as putting strip lights amongst the cobble sets bordering the pond so that at night it looks like a landing strip. Round the side, screened from view, is another 'room' with lawn and a sauna. The colours throughout are kept to grey, green and red. The latter colour was already used inside the house, and was asked for by the owners in their brief, which was for a minimal, symmetrical garden: an instruction exceptionally fulfilled.

Ute does not always get such a clear brief, and amongst her larger projects is another roof garden, where she was given a very free reign. This one is spectacularly situated as part of the redevelopment of a former shipyard, on the north shore of the River Main, in Frankfurt, where tall, modern buildings sit side by side with an old power station. Built over garages, the area Ute designed comprises a terrace with tables and chairs and geometric gardens representing different climate zones. There is a circular Mediterranean garden intersected with stripes of over 14,000 sempervivums planted in gravel, a bamboo garden, and one of grasses and roses.

Ute's temporary installations are also spectacular, for example, her exhibit for the garden festival at Schloss Fasanerie, in Hesse, in 2011. The theme was 'Japan' and Ute used an Asian idea of a tree hung with paper wishes. Her wishes were printed on

white streamers, one metre in length, made of a waterproof material. And her tree, unlike any other, was painted bright, lapis lazuli blue. Ute loves this colour, saying, "It is like fire!" She used ultramarine pigment, mixed with water, to get the particular hue used by Yves Klein (the French artist, 1928–1962) in his monochrome paintings. Having found an old, dead tree near her home, Ute got permission to remove it and then painted it using an airbrush. By the end, she was blue too.

Ute's design for the Hesse festival in 2009 also used blue and was equally arresting. A zigzagging blue wooden walkway was edged on one side with scarlet field poppies. The concept arose because the poppy is a threatened flower and Ute wanted to celebrate the significance of this ancient crop. One capsule holds up to 5,000 tiny seeds and because of that it is thought of as a symbol of fertility and wealth. It has also come to symbolise remembrance. As a medical plant, poppy seeds are calming and painkilling: they are often administered in the case of respiratory diseases, restlessness and insomnia. Since time immemorial the poppy has symbolised long lasting sleep. Vibrant poppy fields have given joy to many, inspired painters, poets and also this garden.

The limited colours and sharp lines here might give a clue to the designer, though this is very different from Ute's own, charmingly crowded, garden. Ute's home garden is the smallest included in this book. But based on possibilities rather than restraints, it bears testament to the fact that a garden does not have to be large to be beautiful or to express personality. Ute sums it up when she says, "It is small but it is my paradise."

STEPHEN **WOODHAMS**

PREVIOUS SPREAD: Stephen has used many of the same techniques as are so skillfully deployed in his own garden for this private client. Even the wooden dog inside is the same.

RIGHT: The line between inside and out almost evaporates here, as style, colour, shapes and even materials are echoed in each.

Stephen Woodhams is famed as much for his floristry as for his garden design, so it is perhaps surprising that instead of traditional English, floriferous gardens, he designs stark, sophisticated, striking outdoor rooms.

Aged sixteen, Stephen gained a place to study at Wisley, the Royal Horticultural Society's garden. He went on to become buyer at the renowned London florists Moyses Stevens. When he was 22 he won a youth enterprise grant and set up his own business in his garden shed. In 1989, Stephen opened his first shop and began establishing his portfolio of celebrity clients for whom he styled parties and weddings. He has been commissioned to create the floral decorations for nine galas at the Royal Opera House in Covent Garden and the inaugural dinner at the Tate Modern gallery.

Running in parallel with Stephen's success in floristry and interior design was his interest in landscape design, which is now the focus of his attention, both in England and on the Spanish island of Ibiza. With his 1994 Chelsea garden (where he was one of the youngest designers ever to win a gold medal), Stephen pioneered the 'inside/outside' concept, and he has been applying interior approaches for outdoor living in cutting-edge gardens ever since. His own garden – a roof terrace atop a former south London transport depot built in the '30s – is no exception.

Stephen's flat is on the second floor, next to his office, which impresses and amazes because everything in it, from furnishing to files, is white. His small apartment (shown here) is mainly grey in colour but not in mood; it is flamboyant and ornate, and the open-plan living area has a magazine-look, with dining table on the right and seating area on the left. Large French windows open onto the 7 x 9 metre roof terrace that duplicates the living space inside, in reverse position. An L-shaped, comfortable seating area round an outdoor fireplace, which doubles as a coffee table, is opposite the indoor dining area. A large dining table and chairs are on the other side. Around the perimeter are six huge, white, plastic pots containing trees and plants. There are also zinc containers for seasonal planting – in spring these are filled with vibrant tulips.

The whole is big, bold and beautiful in a jaw-dropping way. I have never been in a small garden with so much furniture in it, but it did not feel overcrowded. Equally, I have never been in a garden that felt so much like an indoor room, and yet it was imbued with a sense of calm and of nature. Stephen has created a true extension of his flat; an outdoor living area, laid out as you would an interior, so the two merge. The furniture both inside and out is in similar colours and is arranged in grid formation; grey porcelain floor tiles within continue through onto the terrace. Mirrors are a feature in both areas. Sitting at the indoor dining table, the garden is reflected in a large mirror on the side wall; outside, images are duplicated in a mirror on the outer wall of the flat; while sitting on the sofa outside, looking in, the garden is reflected in the splashback in the kitchen.

ABOVE: The inner glass balustrade is far more interesting than if it had been merely added to the outer wall and enhances the spectacle when looking up at the building from below.

OPPOSITE: A wooden dog realistically looks out at the garden, emphasising the ambiguity between indoor and outer spaces.

Stephen has lived here for four years, his decision to buy being totally driven by the outdoor space. When he moved in there was faux pine flooring inside, decking outside and a timber balustrade. He immediately saw the opportunity to design a seamless link between inside and out, so that whilst sitting on the terrace, one can forget that one is outside, thus greatly enlarging the living space. One of Stephen's aims when

designing urban gardens is to try to make both inside and outside spaces seem larger than they really are, using a continuation of materials. In his own garden he was even careful to match up the grouting lines of the tiles so that they flow outwards, extending the flat. Flowers on the indoor dining table are often picked from the garden, as echoes.

Stephen has linked inside and out in the furniture as well. He designed both dining tables in white Carrara marble. He has used interweaving logs of silver birch to form sculptural plinths inside and has used the same lattice formation as the base of the outdoor fireplace. As Stephen points out, "the reason the garden is like it is, is because the interior was designed simultaneously with the garden." In other peoples' gardens he enjoys working with architects and interior designers as a team to produce a similar effect.

The outdoor fireplace uses liquid gas, which gives good heat, and the whole terrace can, on a winter's evening, be covered by a large blind that extends from the house, enabling the garden to be used all year. The chairs, which look as though they could be for indoor use, are, Stephen assures me, left out all year. Hydro cushions are covered with fabric suited to exterior conditions. Silvered, wooden chairs appear to be upholstered in grey velvet. A dark grey rug on the ground is actually plastic grass, which has been specially made (in the Mediterranean, where the light is much stronger, he uses white in his designs).

Woodhams is fascinated by the juxtaposition of new industrial materials combined with traditional techniques and methods. He was one of the first designers to use decking, but also materials that were considered purely utilitarian, such as galvanised steel (introduced by Stephen in the 1990s and still used for his trademark pots),

zinc and Corten steel for containers, metal grille or non-slip metal safety flooring, and glass. Since silicone bonding has eliminated the need for a metal framework, Stephen believes that glass is more versatile. He has used it as an inner wall to his roof terrace (in panels the same width as the floor tiles) with the advantage that, being transparent, it adds the illusion of size and maximises space.

The outer perimeter wall is too low for building regulations to allow the space to be used as a roof garden, so when Stephen got planning permission for the garden, it stipulated that a balustrade had to be installed. He used a high glass wall in front of the brick one, filling the space between with six huge pots, creating an Alice in Wonderland feel. For another of Stephen's loves is over scaling. These plastic pots might be considered far too big, but actually, they too, make the garden appear larger. This idea works well in small gardens of any kind, where a large ornamental feature such as a sculpture or urn, increases the perceived size of the space.

Stephen has used a gloss finish for two of the white plastic pots, which contain olive trees, while the others are matt white. The matt ones have lights under the rim that are colour changeable, meaning that at night the pots can be red, blue, green, yellow or

purple, depending on mood. "In an urban environment I think you can push the barriers", Stephen explains, and continues, "Focused lighting in a garden plays a huge part in evoking atmosphere at night. The lighting here looks like a film set."

Within the pots, Stephen has planted what he calls miniature gardens. Beneath the silver birches are Solomon's seal, hostas, euphorbias and hellebores in a slightly woodland mix. Beneath two olive trees are irises, *Stipa gigantea* and grey-foliaged plants in a more Mediterranean palette. Finally, under the eucalyptus trees, Stephen has planted hebes, acorus and other plants from warmer climes. Each of these three trees has an open habit, allowing the wind to blow through the leaves, reducing the risk of scorching or of the trees being blown over. However, Stephen does not think of plants in isolation, but as one of the many elements that make up an artistic installation.

ABOVE: Mirrors are another way of adding a sense of space.

OPPOSITE: Throughout the garden colours cohere. On this side the white of the table is picked up in the pots and Hyacinth 'White Pearl'.

In the centre of the back wall, in front of the pots, is a square, zinc water feature bubbling away. Water of some kind is usually present in Stephen's gardens, as he likes the sound and the movement. He tries to provide water that, as here, with a self-circulating pump in the base, is low maintenance. This feature is not plumbed into anything and is both easy to install and practical to keep.

Stephen is known for, and mostly asked to design, low-maintenance gardens. He says that as people have less and less free time, they want an outdoor space, but cannot spend long looking after it. His advice is to go for evergreen planting, but he also maintains that however small your budget, you should seek some advice from a designer in order to spend money wisely and choose plants suited to your situation. If you have a roof terrace, weight is an issue, and Stephen points out that sometimes working with a structural surveyor is important, as well as knowing what the load-bearing capacity is. For his own garden, he is right on the limit. He cannot have one more pot and he has to be careful if he has more than six people on the roof. All his plants are in lightweight containers; one third filled with clay granules (for drainage), two-thirds light compost. Everything has been carefully calculated. There is automatic irrigation so that when Stephen is working in his office in Ibiza, he can rest assured that his plants will not suffer.

When in London, Stephen uses the space a lot, feeling it to be a haven. He also enjoys inviting friends over for dinner al fresco. As he says, "I wanted everyone to come round and see the tulips. It is a moment. It is a three-week period that I like to share." The garden is also a place to experiment, even if on a fairly small scale. This year Stephen has got *Tulipa* 'Black Jewel', a sumptuously coloured, fringed variety. Starting maroon-black, to Stephen's surprise and delight it fades to deep rust. Next year he will plant this in a client's garden edged in Corten steel.

Stephen tells me that for him the joy of gardening is that you are always observing and learning. He explains that it was his knowledge of the way things grow that helped with his work with cut flowers, rather than the other way around: "I see things growing and I think, 'Oh! That would look wonderful in a vase'. Or I grow things especially for flower arrangements." He is not tempted to grow more flowers here because, having limited space, he wanted a design that would look beautiful, but also provide a place where he could have friends round for drinks or a meal. As he says, "The garden is about having *life* in it, and that is people, enjoying it."

Stephen admits that in some ways he is lucky because he does not just garden in his own space, but also in other peoples' and can get surrogate pleasure from clients' gardens. His own

ABOVE: Hyacinth 'Woodstock' mingles with fringed *Tulipa* 'Black Jewel', pale-edged *T.* 'Arabian Mystery', and purple *T.* 'Van der Neer'. Together they weave a tapestry of ravishing richness.

OPPOSITE: Movement and sound add further dimensions to this scene of tranquil symmetry.

BELOW: Everything is carefully planned, down to the tulips matching the colour of the tiled roof behind.

garden, he maintains, is exactly the same as it would be if it had been designed for a client. As he puts it, "This has got my handwriting all over it. The garden is a combination of classic and contemporary, which is very much my look." There are modern slatted-wood sofas along with Louis XV-style upholstered chairs. The sheer glass balustrade runs beneath an old brick chimney-breast clothed in wisteria. Colours, too, are a mix of subtle and bold. Whilst the overall impression is of grey, Stephen likes to sometimes shock with orange or lime green, although this year he has opted for luscious hot pink and purple. Fragrance is also important to him, the combination achieved perfectly in Hyacinth 'Woodstock' (a strong-scented garden variety in rich bishop's purple).

Woodhams believes that monochrome plantings can be used to strengthen the framework of a garden and that using large drifts (or in his own case, rows) of one type of plant, with slight variations in colour, can create an impression of wonderful abundance. Sometimes only one or two plant species create a garden that will make a striking impression. Ideas such as these also resonate in his commissioned work.

One such space is a stunning, tiny garden and conservatory filled with brightness and light despite a small, potentially gloomy, location on top of a small, flat-roofed shop. The containorised planting here is green and white – the former coming mainly from evergreens such as bamboo and palms, and the white from seasonal planting of hyacinths followed by busy lizzies, Longi lilies and then white hydrangeas. Conservatory and garden are linked by their use of high-tech materials: metal and

glass, with both floors lit from beneath. The garden is enlivened by metal flooring, seating and containers, with corrugated sheeting and mirror glass, which create a deceptive sense of space. Mirrors are also used in the conservatory, giving the illusion that the garden beyond is never-ending. In the transparent conservatory, the walls and floor are glass, with one additional clear panel of glass in the sandblasted floor, beneath which Stephen placed four rows of ostrich eggs!

Another inspiring London garden that Stephen designed (in collaboration with the architect owner and an interior designer) started off as a wild overgrown orchard. The architecture and views from both the front and rear of the property gave the lead to the style of the outdoor space, and colour was once again co-ordinated (see pp.224-5). The internal floor of cream limestone was also used for the exterior terrace, with pathways

OPPOSITE: This fabulous fusion of garden and conservatory is achieved with a core choice of colours and textures creating a spare yet dynamic whole.

Stephen's recent work is increasingly linear. This striking space, part of a large garden in Majorca, relies on rows of *Echinocactus grusonii*, a line of *Agave Americana,* and a gnarled olive as focal point.

and mulch of Cotswold chippings. Inside, the house was painted in vanilla, with accents of orange, black and lime green, so these same colours were chosen for the planting. As in Baroque music, there is a unifying ground base colour with juxtaposed contrapuntal high notes creating the melody.

Recently Stephen has moved away from concentrating on urban courtyards and roof terraces to design large country gardens both in England and, particularly, abroad. The Mediterranean offers a slower pace of life that he enjoys. Here his designs also have strong architectural identities, with strident structure utilising parallel lines and grids. They, too, showcase elegant planting but tend to include features such as dramatic swimming pools, as well as a different palette of plants. Here Stephen is keen to have a location-based style and adopt a more sustainable approach, with native plants, such as succulents, that require less irrigation. He is also sensitive to light pollution and is more subtle with lighting.

Having new plants with which to design is a bonus to Stephen. In one garden in Majorca he has used barrel cacti almost as art installations. The main spine of the house inside extends out to the whole length of the garden. The house is further divided by five courtyards, where rows of cacti provide sculptural dynamism. Glass, pools and strong light provide reflections for the exotic planting. The colours are largely green with some orange from flowering plants in January and February, when the

clients are at home. Restful grey/green is provided by large olive trees, which were craned onto the site. In another Mediterranean garden, Stephen created a long rill in stone as a main feature, displaying his increasing interest in large, linear landscapes.

All Stephen's gardens, whether big or small, his own or for clients, have a strong sense of design; his are not casual spaces. In fact the same principals apply to his gardens as to his flower arrangements – both pack a punch and are exuberant, but both are ultimately about control. Stephen is a master of manipulation.

FURTHER READING

Amidon, J., *Radical Landscapes: Reinventing Outdoor Space* (Thames & Hudson Ltd., 2001)

Baker, B., *Dream Gardens of England: 100 Inspirational Gardens* (Merrell Publishers Ltd., 2010)

Baker, B., *Why We Garden: Stories of a British Obsession* (Aston House Press, 2004)

Berleant, A., *The Aesthetics of Environment* (Temple University Press, 1995)

Blanc, P., *Gardening Vertically: 24 Ideas for Creating Your Own Green Walls* (W.W. Norton & Co., 2012)

Blanc, P., *The Vertical Garden: In Nature and the City* (W.W. Norton & Co., 2008)

Bradley-Hole, C., *Making the Modern Garden* (Mitchell Beazley, 2007)

Brookes, J. *Room Outside: A New Approach to Garden Design* (Garden Art Press; New Ed., 2007)

Brown, J., *The Modern Garden* (Thames & Hudson Ltd., 2000)

Browning, D., *The New Garden Paradise: Great Private Gardens of the World* (W.W. Norton & Company, 2005)

Cooper, G. and G. Taylor, *Gardens for the Future: Gestures Against the Wild* (Monacelli Press Inc., 2000)

Cooper, G. and G. Taylor, *Mirrors of Paradise: The Gardens of Fernando Caruncho* (Monacelli Press, Inc., 2000)

Cooper, P., *The New Tech Garden* (Mitchell Beazley, 2001)

Dickey, P., *Breaking Ground: Garden Design Solutions from Ten Contemporary Masters* (Artisan, 1997)

Don, M., *Around the World in 80 Gardens* (Weidenfeld & Nicholson, 2008)

Eckbo, G., *Landscape for Living* (University of Massachusetts Press; reprint, 2009)

Falkenberg, H., *Garden Design* (teNeues Publishing Company, 2008)

Fogarty, J. and C. Green, *Australian Inspiration* (Lothian Books, 2004)

Gavin, D. and T. Conran, *Outdoors: The Garden Design Book for the Twenty-First Century* (Conran Octopus Ltd., 2007)

Geuze, A., H. Ibelings and C. Onwuka, *West 8: Mosaics* (Birkhauser Verlag AG, 2007)

Greene, I., *Greene Gardens: The Sustainable Landscape Designs of Isabelle Greene* (Gibbs M. Smith Inc., 2008)

Greene, I., *Shaping Place in the Landscape* (University Art Museum, University of California, 2005)

Guinness, B., M. Biggs, J. Cushnie and B. Flowerdew, *Gardeners' Question Time Plant Chooser* (Kyle Cathie, 2003)

Guinness, B., *Decorative Gardening with Bunny Guinness: Exciting and Fun Projects to Transform Your Garden* (David & Charles Publishers; New Ed., 2005)

Guinness, B., *Family Gardens: How to Create Magical Spaces for All Ages* (David & Charles Publishers; Rev Ed., 2008)

Guinness, B., *Garden Your Way to Health and Fitness* (Timber Press Inc., 2008)

Harte, S., *Zen Gardening* (Pavilion Books Ltd., 1999)

Hobhouse, P., *In Search of Paradise: Great Gardens of the World* (Frances Lincoln Ltd., 2006)

Jellicoe, G., *Modern Private Gardens* (Abelard-Schuman, 1968)

Jones, L., *The Garden Visitor's Companion* (Thames & Hudson Ltd., 2008)

Kingsbury, N., *Gardeners At Home: The Private Spaces of the World's Leading Designers* (Pavilion, 2011)

Lutsko, R., R.S. Menigoz and B. Feller-Roth, *Landscape Plans* (A Ortho Information Services, 1966)

Masuno, S. (Introduction), *The Modern Japanese Garden* (Mitchell Beazley, 2002)

Oudolf, P., *Landscapes in Landscapes* (Monacelli Press Inc., 2011)

Page, R., *The Education of a Gardener* (Collins, 1972)

Papanek, V., *The Green Imperative: Ecology and Ethics in Design and Architecture* (Thames & Hudson, 1995)

Pearson, D., *Home Ground: Sanctuary in the City* (Conran Octopus, 2011)

Pearson, D., *Spirit: Garden Inspiration* (Fuel, 2009)

Pearson, D., *The Garden: A Year at Home Farm* (Ebury Press, 2001)

Pearson, D. and T. Conran, *The Essential Garden Book: The Comprehensive Source Book of Garden Design* (Conran Octapus, 1998)

Phaidon Editors, *The Contemporary Garden* (Phaidon Press Ltd., 2009)

Richardson, T., *Avant Gardeners: 50 Visionaries of the Contemporary Landscape* (Thames & Hudson Ltd., 2008)

Robinson, W., *The Wild Garden* (The Collins Press; New Illustrated. Ed., 2010)

Schroder, T., *Changes in Scenery: Contemporary Landscape Architecture in Europe* (Birkhauser Verlag AG; 2nd Revised Ed., 2002)

Street-Porter, T., *Tropical Houses: Living in Natural Paradise* (Thames & Hudson Ltd., 2000)

Strong, R., *Gardens Through the Ages* (Conran Octopus Ltd.; New Ed., 2000)

Stuart-Smith, T. and S. Stuart-Smith, *The Barn Garden: Making a Place* (Serge Hill Books, 2011)

Sturgeon, A., *Big Plans, Small Gardens* (Mitchell Beazley, 2010)

Sturgeon, A., *Planted* (Hodder & Stoughton Ltd.; New Ed., 1999)

Taylor, P., *The Wirtz Gardens* (BAI NV.; 2004)

White, Hazel *Small Tree Gardens* (Chronicle Books, 2000)

Wijaya, M., *Architecture of Bali: A Sourcebook of Traditional and Modern Forms* (Thames & Hudson, 2011)

Wijaya, M., *At Home in Bali* (Abbeville Press Inc., 2000)

Wijaya, M., *Modern Tropical Garden Design* (Thames & Hudson, 2007)

Wilson, A., *Influential Gardeners: The Designers Who Shaped 20th-Century Garden Style* (Mitchell Beazley, 2002)

Woodhams, S., *Flowers* (Quadrille Publishing Ltd., 2004)

Woodhams, S., *Portfolio of Contemporary Gardens* (Quadrille Publishing Ltd.; New Ed., 2001)

PICTURE CREDITS

Barbara Baker: pages 6, 9 (above), 10-11, 12-13, 14 (above), 15 (both), 16-17, 18, 20, 51, 56 (both), 57, 59, 91, 93 (below), 96, 132, 133 (above left), 134-5, 152 (both), 153, 154, 155 (below), 175, 176-7, 184, 185, 208 (both), 214-5, 216, 219 (above), 222, 226-7, 228, 229, 230, 231, 232, 233 (both)

Robin Baker: pages 7, 9 (below), 30, 54-5, 58 (both), 60, 86-7, 88-9 (both), 90, 92, 93 (above left and right), 113, 114-5 (both), 118, 119, 120, 121, 133 (below left and right), 137, 142, 143, 168, 169, 170, 171, 172, 174, 178, 179, 180, 181, 183, 200-1, 209, 212-3, 217, 218, 219 (below), 220-1

Patrick Blanc: pages 14 (below), 21

Marion Brenner: pages 74-5, 76, 77 (both), 78. 79, 80, 81, 82, 83, 85, 106, 107, 108-9

Nicola Browne: pages 161 (above left and right), 162

Nate Cervantes: pages 102 (both), 103, 104-5

Kate Cullity: page 36 (right)

Jim Fogarty: pages 44-5, 46, 47, 48, 49, 50, 52, 53

Trevor Fox: pages 34-5

© **Ludwig Gerns:** pages 61, 62, 63

Ricardo Gómez-Acebo: page 26 (below)

Raúl Tomás Granizo: pages 22-3, 28-9, 31

Bunny Guinness: pages 94 (below left), 94-5

Gil Hanly: page 163

Grant Hancock: page 41

Jerry Harpur: pages 26 (above right), 27, 187

Hirota Haruo: pages 110-11, 116-7

Peter Hyatt: pages 32-3, 40

Edward James: page 42

Veronique Lalot: page 19

Andrew Lawson: pages 166-7, 173

Jason Liske: pages 100, 101, 105 (right)

Marianne Majeras: page 97

Huw Morgan: pages 122-3, 124-5, 127, 128, 129

Syogo Oizumi / Tokachi Millennium Forest: pages 130, 131

Heiner Orth: pages 224-5, 235

Matthew Page: pages 146-7, 151, 155 (above)

Antonio Perazzi: pages 136, 138, 139, 140, 141, 144, 145 (both)

Pere Planells: pages 24-5

© **Quilted Velvet:** page 150 (both)

Andy Rusheed: pages 36 (left), 38, 39, 43

Madeleine Marie Slavick: pages 156-7, 158, 159, 161 (below), 164-5

Karen Smith: page 148

Tim Street-Porter: pages 188-9, 190, 192, 193, 196

Andy Sturgeon: page 186

Neil Tinning: page 149

Juliette Wade: page 94 (above left)

© **West 8 Urban Design and Landscape Art:** pages 64-5, 66 (both), 67, 68, 69, 70, 71, 72-3

Made Wijaya: pages 194-5, 197, 198, 199

© **2006 Steve Wittaker, with thanks to Trilogy Architects, The McConnell Foundation and Lutsko Associates:** pages 98-9

© **Wirtz International nv:** pages 202-3, 204, 205, 206, 207, 210-11

Ute Wittich: 223 (both)

Andrew Wood: page 234

Ben Wrigley: page 37

Diter Zoern: page 26 (above left)

INDEX

*Page numbers in **bold** refer to images.*